THE

MASTER·SINGERS

OF

NUREMBERG.

(DIE MEISTERSINGER VON NÜRNBERG.)

OPERA IN THREE ACTS,

BY

RICHARD WAGNER.

WITH GERMAN AND ENGLISH WORDS, AND THE MUSIC OF THE PRINCIPAL AIRS.

OLIVER DITSON COMPANY
THEODORE PRESSER CO., DISTRIBUTORS
1712 CHESTNUT STREET
✦ PHILADELPHIA ✦

CHARACTERS.

HANS SACHS, Cobbler		BASS
VEIT POGNER, Goldsmith		"
KUNZ VOGELGESANG, Furrier		TENOR
KONRAD NACHTIGAL, Buckle-maker		BASS
SIXTUS BECKMESSER, Town-Clerk		"
FRITZ KOTHNER, Baker	Master-Singers.	"
BALTHAZAR ZORN, Pewterer		TENOR
ULRIC EISSLINGER, Grocer		"
AUGUSTUS MOSER, Tailor		"
HERMANN ORTEL, Soap-boiler		BASS
HANS SCHWARZ, Stocking-weaver		"
HANS FOLTZ, Coppersmith		"

SIR WALTER VON STOLZING, a young Franconian Knight . . . . TENOR
DAVID, apprentice to Hans Sachs . . . . "
EVA, Pogner's daughter . . . . SOPRANO
MAGDALENA, Eva's nurse . . . . "
A NIGHT-WATCHMAN . . . . BASS

Burghers of all Guilds, Journeymen, Prentices, Girls, and People.

SCENE — Nuremberg in the middle of the 16th Century.

PREFACE.

"Die Meistersinger von Nürnberg" is the eighth in order of Wagner's published operas.

Some acquaintance with the history of the Master-singers of Germany, their manners and customs, and their technical phraseology, is indispensable for a due appreciation of much which would otherwise appear strange and incomprehensible in the text of this opera. The subject being one which has not been made readily accessible to English readers, it seems imperative that an English version of the work should not go forth to the world unaccompanied by some few elucidatory remarks.

The Master-singers are not to be regarded as mythical personages or as emanations of Wagner's brain, as certain of his critics have fondly imagined, but were real flesh and blood. Impossible as it often is to assign a boundary to the different periods of literary history, it is within the mark to assert that Master-singing is most properly to be regarded as the eventual outcome of Minne-singing, and that the culture of poetic art, which in the twelfth and thirteenth centuries belonged exclusively to the Minne-singers, in the fourteenth and four following centuries devolved upon the Master-singers. The Minne-singers, it should be borne in mind, were mostly of noble birth, and lived in kings' houses or wandered about from court to court; the Master-singers, on the other hand, belonged to the burgher and artisan class. Heinrich von Meissen, surnamed Frauenlob, who died in 1318, is generally looked upon as the founder of their schools and guilds. From his time verse-craft became one of the incorporated trades in nearly all German cities, and the burghers obtained the freedom of it as of any other corporation. The aims of the Master-singers' schools and guilds were strictly moral; by the culture and improvement of poetry, and by the discipline which their rules imposed, they sought to raise the mental and moral standard of their youth. But, ascribing an extravagant antiquity to their institutions, placing form above matter, and hedging themselves about with hard and fast rules, the Master-singers arrogated to themselves an undue importance. It is the conceit arising from this,

their sacrifice of matter to form, their pedantry and their conventionalism, that Wagner has sought to satirize in this opera.

In Nuremberg the principal meetings of the Master-singers were held in the Church of St. Catharine after afternoon service on Sundays and Holydays. For an insight into the constitution of their guilds and schools, their rules and regulations, reference is due to the "Schulordnung" or "Lagerbuch," and to the "Tabulatur." The one regulated the discipline and business of their organization, the other its artistic side. The singing at their sittings was divided into "Freisingen" (free singing) and "Hauptsingen" (principal singing). In the former, anyone, even a stranger, might take part; in the latter, which was competitive, the faults against the rules committed by the singer were noted on a slate by a "Merker" (marker) ensconced behind a curtain. Seven faults were allowed, and he who exceeded this number was declared "outsung" and "outdone" ("versungen und verthan"). The candidate for admission into a guild was obliged to find vouchers for his respectability, and had also to undergo the ordeal of singing before the members. If the Marker declared that he had complied with the rules and regulations he was decorated with a silver chain and badge—the latter representing King David playing upon the harp—and was honorably admitted into the guild.

Candidates for admission into a guild, and the younger members thereof, were apprenticed to and instructed free of cost by the elder members, who held the rank of Masters. The members of a guild were thus classified: He who had only partially mastered the "Tabulatur" was called a "Schüler" (scholar); he who had completely familiarized himself with it was a "Schulfreund" (schoolman); he who could sing some half-dozen tunes was a "Singer;" he who could make verses to a given tune was a "Poet"; and he who could invent a new scheme of verse and a new tune was dubbed a "Master."

The "Tabulatur" consisted of rules and prohibitions. The different modes of rhyming were thus defined therein:

Monosyllabic rhymes were called "stumpfe;" dissyllabic "klingende." "Waisen" were rhymeless lines; "Körner" were lines rhyming with one in the following stanza. "Pausen" were monosyllabic words constituting an entire line and rhyming with another similarly situated; dissyllables thus positioned were called "Schlagreime." Thirty-three "Feller" (faults) which were to be guarded against were specified: e. g., a single line might not contain more than thirteen syllables, because more could not be sung in a single breath. A singer must be careful to choose a key within the register of his voice. Among the faults were "blinde Meinung" (clouded meaning, i. e., the omission of conjunctions); "falsch Gebänd" (faulty versification); "unredbare Wörter" (unsingable phrases); "Klebsilbe" (word clippings, i. e., the contraction of two syllables into one); "Laster" (vices, i. e., faulty rhymes) "Aequivoca" (words of a double meaning); "Differenz" (the displacement of the letters in a word, etc.).

The poems of the Master-singers were always lyrical, and generally sung to a given tune. The length of the verse, the number of the lines, and the order of the rhymes being variable, their poems were susceptible of a great variety of forms. "Töne" (tones) denoted the scheme of versification; "Weisen" (modes), the melodies to which they were sung. There were some hundreds of these tones and modes, each of which had its particular title. The Masters were bound to know not only their titles, but to be able to sing them. The construction of a Master-song was governed by fixed rules. The scheme on which it was based was called a "Bar" (stave) and was divided into three or more "Gesätze" (stanzas). Each "Gesätz" consisted generally of two "Stollen" (shorter stanzas) in the same metre, and sung to the same tune. The first "Gesätz" was followed by an "Abgesang" (after-song), differing in metre and in length from the preceding stanzas, and sung to a different melody. The "Abgesang" was sometimes supplemented by another "Gesätz" in the same metre as the first. A complete Master-song generally consisted of three such "staves."

Of the circumstances which led to the choice of the Master-singers as the subject for an opera, Wagner has himself told us in a pamphlet entitled "Eine Mittheilung an meine Freunde" (A Communication to my Friends), first published in 1851. As the account he therein gives is both interesting in itself and at the same time furnishes a sketch of the plot of the opera, it seems best to reproduce it here, as far as translation will allow, in his own words. Wagner writes:—

"Immediately after the conclusion of 'Tannhäuser' (in 1845), I was fortunate in being able to visit a Bohemian bathing-place for the benefit of my health. Here, as on all occasions when I have been able to withdraw myself from the air of the 'footlights,' and from my official duties in such an atmosphere, I soon felt myself in a light and joyous mood. For the first time, and with artistic significance, a gaiety peculiar to my character manifested itself within me. Almost without premeditation I had a

short time previously resolved that my next should be a comic opera. I recall that this determination resulted principally from the advice of well-meaning friends, who wished me to write an opera in a 'lighter style,' because this, they said, would procure my admission to the German theatres, and thus insure that success for the continued want of which my outward circumstances had been seriously threatened.

"As among the Athenians of old a tragedy was followed by a merry satirical piece, there suddenly appeared to me during this journey for my health the picture of a comic play, which might suitably be made to serve as a satirical supplement for my 'Battle of the Bards at the Wartburg.' This was 'Die Meistersinger von Nürnburg,' with Hans Sachs at their head. I conceived Hans Sachs as the last example of the artistically productive folk's-spirit, and in this relation I opposed him to the narrow-mindedness of Master-singer-like Burgherdom, to the extremely droll and tabulatur-poetical pedantry of which I gave a personal expression in the character of the 'Marker.' This 'Marker' as every one knows, or as perhaps our critics did not know, was the overseer appointed by the Singers' Guild to 'mark' with strokes the faults against the rules committed by the executants, especially if they were candidates for admission to the Guild. Whoever got a certain number of strokes against him had 'versungen,' i. e., had failed in his singing.

"Now the eldest of the Guild offered the hand of his young daughter to the Master who, at an approaching public singing-match, should win the prize. The Marker, who has already been paying his addresses to the maiden, finds a rival in the person of a young knight, who, inspired by reading the 'Book of Heroes' and the old Minne-singers, has left the poverty-stricken and decaying castle of his ancestors with a view to learning in Nuremberg the art of the Master-singers. He announces his wish to be admitted into the Guild, being prompted thereto by a passion which he has suddenly conceived for the prize-maiden, 'whom only a Master of the Guild may win.' On putting himself up for examination he sings an enthusiastic song in praise of women, which so repeatedly arouses the disapprobation of the Marker that, before he has half got through it, he has 'failed in his singing.' Sachs, who is pleased with the young man, frustrates, with a view to his welfare, a desperate attempt to carry off the maiden. In doing this he at the same time finds an opportunity of grievously offending the Marker. The latter, who has already been speaking rudely to Sachs with the view of humbling him about a pair of shoes which he has still left unfinished, stations himself at night under the maiden's window, in order to make trial of the song with which he hopes to win her by singing it to her as a serenade, it being his object to secure her voice in his favor in the adjudication of the prize. Sachs, whose workshop is opposite the house thus besung, begins singing loudly just as the Marker has commenced his serenade, because, as he tells the Marker, who is enraged at his doing so, it is necessary to keep himself awake when he has to work so late, and that the work is wanted in a hurry nobody knows better than the Marker, who has pressed him so hardly for it. At last he promises the luckless fellow to give over singing, but on condiction of his being allowed to mark also in his manner — as a shoemaker — the faults which, according to his feelings, he may find in the Marker's song, viz., by a stroke of his hammer for each fault upon the shoe stretched upon the last. The Marker sings; Sachs strikes the last again and again. In a passion the Marker jumps up; Sachs coolly asks him if he has finished his song. 'Not nearly' he shouts. Sachs, now laughing, holds up the shoes outside his shop, and declares that they are now quite finished, thanks to the ' Marker's taps.' With the rest of his song, which in despair he screams out without a pause, the Marker makes a miserable failure in the presence of the female figure which is seen violently shaking her head at the window. Disconsolate at this, he begs Sachs the following day to furnish him with a new song for his wooing. Sachs accordingly gives him a poem by the young knight, pretending that he does not know from whence it has come. He advises him, however, to make sure of having an appropriate tune to sing it to. The conceited Marker fancies he is all right in this respect, and accordingly sings the poem before the public assembly of the Masters and people to a tune which is thoroughly unsuited to it, and so disfigures it that, once more, and this time decisively, he fails entirely. Enraged thereat, he accuses Sachs of having played him a mean trick in thus foisting upon him so ignominious a poem. Sachs declares that the poem is an exceedingly good one, only it requires to be sung to an appropriate tune. It is then determined that he who knows the proper tune shall be adjudged the victor. The young knight accomplishes this and wins his bride, but rejects with scorn the offer now made him of admission into the Guild. Sachs humourously stands up in defence of the Master-singers' Guild, and finishes with the rhyme :

> " ' Though holy Rome herself should pass away,
>   Our glorious German Art will ne'er decay.' "

The sketch which Wagner at once drew up was not, however, destined to be carried out in the rapid manner in which it was conceived. First, " Lohengrin " engrossed his attention ; then the " Death of Siegfried," which eventually grew into the " Nibelung " tetralogy; and then " Tristan und Isolde." " Die Meistersinger " which must therefore have occupied his thoughts, more or less, for nearly a quarter of a century, was not completed till 1867. It was brought to a public hearing for the first time in the course of the following year, under the direction of Hans von Bulow, at Munich.

As a comical pendant to " Tannhäuser," though not so satirical a one of the Master-singers as Wagner originally intended it to be, " Die Meistersinger " is not without its analogy to this. In " Tannhäuser " it is the victory of virtue over vice that is typified ; " Die Meistersinger " represents the victory of genius, aided by good sense, over pedantry and conventionalism. The moral sought to be conveyed is this : that Art is progressive, and that rules are useful, and are only to be broken by those who have learned to observe them.   C. A. B.

THE MASTER-SINGERS OF NUREMBURG.
(DIE MEISTERSINGER VON NÜRNBERG.)

ACT FIRST.

The scene represents the interior of St. Katherine's church, in oblique section; only the last few rows of pews in the nave — which is supposed to extend out L towards the back — are visible; the foreground is the open space before the choir; this is afterwards shut off by a black curtain from the nave.

As the curtain rises the people are singing, to organ accompaniment, the last verse of a Chorale, which concludes afternoon service on the vigil of the Feast of St. John.

Hymn of the People.
When to thee our Saviour went
To receive thy Sacrament,
Ere His sacrifice divine,
We were giv'n salvation's sign,
That through Baptism we might prove
Worthy of His death and love.
    Interceder,
    Christ's preceder!
    Take us gently o'er
    Unto Jordan's shore.

(During the Chorale and its interludes the following dumb show takes place, accompanied by the orchestra: —
In the last pew are seated Eva and Magdalena; Walter v. Stolzing is leaning against a pillar at a little distance, his eyes fixed on Eva. Eva turns repeatedly towards the knight and answers his now importunate, now tender glances of entreaty and passion shyly and modestly, but tenderly and encouragingly. Magdalena often breaks off her singing to give Eva a reproving nudge. — When the hymn is ended and while, during a long postlude on the organ, the congregation is gradually leaving by the principal door (supposed to be L at back), Walter advances hastily towards Eva and her companion, who have also risen from their seats and turned to go.)

Walter.
        (Softly but ardently to Eva.)
Oh stay! — One word, I do entreat!

Eva.
        (Quickly turning to Magdalena.)
My kerchief! Look! 'T is on the seat!

Magdalena.
Forgetful child! Now here's a hunt!
        (Goes back to the pew.)

ERSTER AUFZUG.

Die Bühne stellt das Innere der Katharinenkirche, in schrägem Durchschnitt, dar; von dem Haupstschiff, welches links ab dem Hintergrunde zu sich ausdehnend anzunehmen ist, sind nur noch die letzten Reihen der Kirchenstühlbänke sichtbar; den Vordergrund nimmt der freie Raum vor dem Chor ein; dieser wird später durch einen Vorhang gegen das Schiff zu gänzlich abgeschlossen.

Beim Aufzug hört man, unter Orgelbegleitung, von der Gemeinde den letzten Vers eines Chorals, mit welchem der Nachmittagsgottesdienst zur Einleitung des Johannisfestes schliesst, singen.

Choral der Gemeinde.
Da zu dir der Heiland kam,
Willig deine Taufe nahm,
Weihte sich dem Opfertod,
Gab er uns des Heil's Gebot:
Dass wir durch dein' Tauf' uns weih'n,
Seines Opfers werth zu sein.
    Edler Täufer,
    Christ's Vorläufer!
Nimm uns freundlich an,
Dort am Fluss Jordan.

(Während des Chorales und dessen Zwischenspielen, entwickelt sich, vom Orchester begleitet, folgende pantomimische Scene.
In der letzten Reihe der Kirchenstühle sitzen Eva und Magdalene; Walther v. Stolzing steht, in einiger Entfernung, zur Seite an eine Säule gelehnt, die Blicke auf Eva heftend. Eva kehrt sich wiederholt seitwärts nach dem Ritter um, und erwiedert seine bald dringend, bald zärtlich durch Gebärden sich ausdrückenden Bitten und Betheuerungen schüchtern und verschämt, doch seelenvoll und ermuthigend. Magdalene unterbricht sich öfter im Gesang, um Eva zu zupfen und zur Vorsicht zu mahnen. — Als der Choral zu Ende ist, und, während eines längeren Orgelnachspieles, die Gemeinde dem Hauptausgange, welcher links dem Hintergrunde zu anzunehmen ist, sich zuwendet, um allmählich die Kirche zu verlassen, tritt Walther an die beiden Frauen, welche sich ebenfalls von ihren Sitzen erhoben haben, und dem Ausgange sich zuwenden wollen, lebhaft heran.)

Walther.
        (Leise, doch feurig zu Eva.)
Verweilt! — Ein Wort! Ein einzig Wort!

Eva.
        (Sich rasch zu Magdalene wendend.)
Mein Brusttuch! Schau! Wohl liegt's im Ort?

Magdalene.
Vergesslich Kind! Nun heisst es: such'!
        (Sie kehrt nach den Sitzen zurück.)

Walter. Maiden, forgive if I affront—
One thing to ask you, one to discover,
What rules would I not dare pass over?
Is life for me or death?—Is bliss for me or
   bane?
Thy answer let in one word be clothed:
Fair maiden, say—

Magdalena.
(Returning.)
Here 't is again!

Eva. Alack! my scarf-pin! . . .

Magdalena. Did it fall out?
(She goes back, searching on the ground.)

Walter.
Is 't light and laughter, or gloom and doubt?
Can I attain the aim I approach to,
Or must I hear the syllable loathed—
Fair maiden, say—

Magdalena.
(Returning again.)
I have found the brooch, too!
Come, child, here 's pin and 'kerchief, look!
Good lack! if I 've not forgot my book!
(Goes back once more.)

Walter. This single word, you speak it not—
This syllable that casts my lot?
Say Yes or No,—'t is quickly mouthed:
Fair maiden, say, are you betrothed?

Magdalena.
(Who has returned again, curtsies to Walter.)
Sir knight, your servant!
This is a compliment!
Our Eva's escort
Do you then represent?
Pray, Master Pogner is it
Your worship seeks to visit?

Walter.
(Sorrowfully.)
Would I never his house had seen!

Magdalena.
Hey day, sir! why, what do you mean?
When unto Nuremberg first you wended
Was not his friendly hand extended?
The bed and board, the dishes, drinks
He gave deserve some thanks, methinks?

Eva.
Good Lena! Pray! He meant it not so:
He is only eager to know—

Walther.
Fräulein! Verzeih't der Sitte Bruch!
Eines zu wissen, Eines zu fragen,
Was nicht müsst' ich zu brechen wagen!
Ob Leben oder Tod? Ob Segen oder Fluch?
Mit einem Worte sei mir's vertraut:—
Mein Fräulein, sagt—

Magdalene.
(Zurückkommend.)
Hier ist das Tuch.

Eva. O weh! die Spange?

Magdalene. Fiel sie wohl ab?
(Sie geht, am Boden suchend, wieder zurück.)

Walther.
Ob Licht und Lust, oder Nacht und Grab?
Ob ich erfahr', wonach ich verlange,
Ob ich vernehme, wovor mir graut.—
Mein Fräulein, sagt . . .

Magdalene.
(Wieder zurückkommend.)
Da ist auch die Spange.—
Komm' Kind! Nun hast du Spang' und
   Tuch.—
O weh! da vergass ich selbst mein Buch!
(Sie kehrt wieder um.)

Walther.
Dies eine Wort, ihr sagt mir's nicht?
Die Sylbe, die mein Urtheil spricht?
Ja, oder: Nein!—ein flücht'ger Laut:
Mein Fräulein, sagt, seid ihr schon Braut?

Magdalene.
(Die bereits zurückgekommen, verneigt sich vor
   Walther.)
Sieh da, Herr Ritter?
Wie sind wir hochgeehrt:
Mit Evchen's Schutze
Habt ihr euch gar beschwert?
Darf den Besuch des Helden
Ich Meister Pogner melden?

Walther.
(Leidenschaftlich.)
Betrat ich doch nie sein Haus!

Magdalene.
Ei! Junker! Was sagt ihr da aus!
In Nürnberg eben nur angekommen,
War't ihr nicht freundlich aufgenommen?
Was Küch' und Keller, Schrein und Schrank
Euch bot, verdient' es keinen Dank?

Eva.
Gut' Lenchen! Ach! das meint er ja nicht.
Doch wohl von mir wünscht er Bericht—

How shall I say? — I scarce comprehend —
His words my senses nearly suspend! —
He asks — about my choice!

Magdalena.
(Looking about apprehensively.)
Oh lud! subdue your voice!
Come directly home with me,
Just suppose the folks should see!

Walter. Not yet, till I know my fate!

Eva. They 're gone, there 's no one nigh.

Magdalena. That 's why I 'm in a state!
Sir knight, pray elsewhere try!

(David enters from the sacristy and busies himself with
drawing together dark curtains which are so disposed as
to close off the foreground of the stage from the nave.)

Walter. Nay! your reply?

Eva.
(Holding Magdalena.)
Reply?

Magdalena.
(Who has turned away, perceives David, pauses and
calls tenderly aside.)
David! Why, can it be?

Eva.
(Urgently.)
What answer? Speak for me!

Magdalena.
(Distracted in her attention, looking round repeatedly
at David.)
Chevalier, what of this maid you ask
To answer is no easy task:
She is betrothed, you might expect —

Eva.
(Quickly interrupting.)
But none has seen the bridegroom elect.

Magdalena.
The groom, in sooth, will not be known
Until to-morrow by trial shewn,
When a Master-Singer receives the prize —

Eva.
(As before.)
And my own hand his bay-wreath ties.

Walter. A Master-Singer?

Eva.
(Timidly.)
Are you not one?

Wie sag' ich's schnell? — Versteh' ich's noch
kaum! —
Mir ist, als wär' ich gar wie im Traum! —
Er frägt, — ob ich schon Braut?

Magdalene.
(Sich scheu umsehend.)
Hilf Gott! Sprich nich so laut!
Jetzt lass' uns nach Hause gehn;
Wenn uns die Leut' hier sehn!

Walther. Nicht eher, bis ich Alles weiss!

Eva. 's ist leer, die Leut' sind fort.

Magdalene.
D'rum eben wird mir heiss! —
Herr Ritter, an andrem Ort!

(David tritt aus der Sacristei ein und macht sich darüber
her, dunkle Vorhänge, welche so angebracht sind, dass sie
den Vordergrund der Bühne nach dem Kirchenschiff zu
schräg abschliessen, aneinander zu ziehen.)

Walther. Nein! Erst dies Wort?

Eva.
(Magdalene haltend.)
Dies Wort!

Magdalene.
(Die sich bereits umgewendet, erblickt David, hält an
und ruft zärtlich für sich.)
David? Ei! David hier!

Eva.
(Drängend.)
Was sag' ich? Sag' du's mir!

Magdalene.
(Mit Zerstreutheit, öfters nach David sich umsehend.)
Herr Ritter, was ihr die Jungfer fragt,
Das ist so leichtlich nicht gesagt:
Fürwahr ist Evchen Pogner Braut —

Eva.
(Schnell unterbrechend.)
Doch hat noch Keiner den Bräut'gam er
schaut.

Magdalene.
Den Bräut'gam wohl noch Niemand kennt,
Bis morgen ihn das Gericht ernennt,
Das dem Meistersinger ertheilt den Preis —

Eva.
(Wie zuvor.)
Und selbst die Braut ihm reicht das Reis.

Walther. Dem Meistersinger?

Eva.
(Bang.)
Seid ihr das nicht?

Walter. A trial-song?

Magdalena. 'Fore judges done.

Walter. Who wins the prize?

Magdalena. 'T is for them to shew one.

Walter. The bride will choose—?

Eva.
(Forgetting herself.)
You, or else no one!

(Walter turns aside in great perturbation, pacing up and down.)

Magdalena.
(Greatly shocked.)
Why, Eva! Eva! Are you insane?

Eva. Good Lena! Help me my lover to gain!

Magdalena.
Yesterday first did you see his face.

Eva. Kindled my love at so swift a pace
Having his portrait so oft in sight.
Say, is he not like David quite?

Magdalena. Are you mad? Like David?

Eva. The picture, I mean.

Magdalena. Oh! he with the harp and beard
long flowing,
As on the Masters' escutcheon seen?

Eva.
Nay! he Goliath with pebble o'erthrowing,
With sword at side and sling in hand,
Light locks surrounding his head like rays,
As Master Albrecht Dürer portrays.

Magdalena.
(Sighing loudly.)
Ah! David! David!

David.
(Who has gone out, now returns with a rule stuck in his girdle, and swinging in his hand a large piece of chalk tied to a string.)
Here am I! who calls?

Magdalena.
Ah, David! throu̶h thee what ill befalls!
(Aside.)
The darling rogue! he knows it, too!
(Aloud.)
Why, look! he 's shut us all up inside here!

David.
(Tenderly to Magdalena.)
But *you* in my heart!

Walther. Ein Werbgesang?

Magdalene. Vor Wettgericht.

Walther. Den Preis gewinnt?

Magdalene. Wen die Meister meinen.

Walther. Die Braut dann wählt?

Eva.
(Sich vergessend.)
Euch, oder Keinen!
(Walther wendet sich, in grosser Aufregung auf und abgehend, zur Seite.)

Magdalene.
(Sehr erschrocken.)
Was? Evchen! Evchen! Bist du von
Sinnen?

Eva.
Gut' Lene! hilf mir den Ritter gewinnen!

Magdalene.
Sah'st ihn doch gestern zum ersten Mal?

Eva. Das eben schuf mir so schnelle Qual,
Dass ich schon längst ihn im Bilde sah;
Sag', trat er nicht ganz wie David nah'?

Magdalene. Bist du toll? Wie David?

Eva. Wie David im Bild.

Magdalene.
Ach! meinst du den König mit der Harfen,
Und langem Bart in der Meister Schild?

Eva.
Nein! der, dess' Kiesel den Goliath warfen,
Das Schwert im Gurt, die Schleuder zur
Hand,
Von lichten Locken das Haupt umstrahlt,
Wie ihn uns Meister Dürer gemalt.

Magdalene.
(Laut seufzend.)
Ach, David! David!

David.
(Der herausgegangen und jetzt wieder zurückkommt, ein Lineal im Gürtel und ein grosses Stück weisser Kreide an einer Schnur in der Hand schwenkend.)
Da bin ich! Wer ruft?

Magdalene.
Ach, David! Was ihr für Unglück schuft!
(Für sich.)
Der liebe Schelm! wüsst' er's noch nicht?
(Laut.)
Ei, seht! da hat er uns gar verschlossen?

David.
(Zärtlich zu Magdalene.)
In's Herz euch allein!

Magdalena.
    (Aside.)
        His face is so true!
    (Aloud.)
Come, say! what frolic's to be tried here?

David. Forefend it! Frolic? A serious thing!
For the Masters I'm preparing the ring.

Magdalena. What! will there be singing?

David.   A trial mere:
That Prentice wins his enfranchisement
Who ne'er gained for breach of the rules chastisement;
He who passes is Master here.

Magdalena.
Then the knight has dropped on the proper spot.
Now, Evy, come, we ought to trot.

Walter.
    (Quickly turning to them.)
To Master Pogner let me escort you.

Magdalena.
Await his approach; he'll be here soon.
If to win our Eva sought you,
Both time and place were opportune.
    (Two Prentices enter, bearing benches.)
    Quick! bid us adieu!

Walter. What must I do?

Magdalena. Let David supply all
    The facts of the trial.—
David, my dear, just heed what I say!
You must induce Sir Walter to stay.
    The larder I'll sweep,
    The best for you keep;
To-morrow rewards shall fall faster
If this young knight is made Master.
    (She hurries towards the door.)

Eva.
    (To Walter.)
When shall I see you?

Walter.
    (Ardently.)
      This evening, for sure!
What use declaring
How great my daring?
New is my heart, new my mind,
New to my senses is all I find,
    One thing I spring to,
    One thing I cling to;

Magdalene.
    (Bei Seite.)
      Das treue Gesicht!—
    (Laut.)
Nein sagt! Was treibt ihr hier für Possen?

David.
Behüt' es! Possen! Gar ernste Ding'?
Für die Meister hier richt' ich den Ring.

Magdalene. Wie? Gäb' es ein Singen?

David.   Nur Freiung heut':
Der Lehrling wird da losgesprochen,
Der nichts wider die Tabulatur verbrochen:
Meister wird, wen die Prob' nicht reu't.

Magdalene.
Da wär' der Ritter ja am rechten Ort.—
Jetzt, Evchen, komm', wir müssen fort.

Walther.
    (Schnell sich zu den Frauen wendend.)
Zu Meister Pogner lasst mich euch geleiten.

Magdalene.
Erwartet den hier: er ist bald da.
Wollt ihr euch Evchen's Hand erstreiten,
Rückt Ort und Zeit das Glück euch nah'.
    (Zwei Lehrbuben kommen dazu und tragen Bänke.)
    Jetzt eilig von hinnen!

Walther.
    Wass soll ich beginnen?

Magdalene.
    Lasst David euch lehren
    Die Freiung begehren.—
Davidchen! hör', mein lieber Gesell,
Den Ritter bewahr' hier wohl zur Stell'!
    Was Fein's aus der Küch'
    Bewahr' ich für dich:
Und morgen begehr' du noch dreister,
Wird heut' der Junker hier Meister.
    (Sie drängt fort.)

Eva.
    (Zu Walther.)
Seh' ich euch wieder?

Walther.
    (Feurig.)
      Heut' Abend, gewiss!—
    Was ich will wagen,
    Wie könnt' ich's sagen!
Neu ist mein Herz, neu mein Sinn,
Neu ist mir Alles, was ich beginn'.
    Eines nur weiss ich,
    Eines begrief' ich:

The hope sustaining
Thy hand of gaining!
Though to obtain thee my sword avail not,
As Master-Singer surely I 'll fail not.
For thee gold untold!
For thee
Poet's courage bold!

Eva.

(With great warmth.)
My heart's secret fold
For thee
Loving heed doth hold!

Magdalena   Quick, home, or shall scold!

David.

(Measuring Walter.)
A Master? Oho! you 're bold!

(Magdalena pulls Eva quickly away through the curtains.
Walter, disturbed and brooding, has thrown himself
upon a raised ecclesiastical arm-chair which two Prentices
had just moved away from the wall to the middle of the
stage.

More Prentices enter; they bring and arrange benches
and prepare everything (during the following dialogue)
for the sitting of the Master-Singers.)

First Prentice.   David, why skulk?

Second Prentice.   Work apace!

Third Prentice.
The Marker's platform help us place!

David.   My labor and industry shame ye:
   Work by yourselves; my own affairs claim
   me!

Second Prentice.   What airs he takes!

Third Prentice.   A model Prentice!

First Prentice.
His time to a shoemaker lent is.

Third Prentice.
His last and pen he holds together.

Second Prentice.
While cobbling he writes his stuff.

First Prentice.
He scribbles verses on scarlet leather.

Third Prentice.
(With expressive gesture.)
We'll soon give him tanning enough!
(They pursue their work, laughing.)

David.
(After observing the meditating knight awhile, calls
loudly):
   "Now, begin!"

Mit allen Sinnen
Euch zu gewinnen!
Ist's mit dem Schwert nicht, mus es gelingen,
Gilt es als Meister euch zu ersingen.
Für euch Gut und Blut!
Für euch
Ditchter's heil'ger Muth!

Eva.

(Mit grosser Wärme.)
Mein Herz, sel'ger Gluth,
Für euch
Liebesheil'ge Huld!

Magdalene.
Schnell heim, sonst geht's nicht gut!

David.

(Walther messend.)
Gleich Meister? Oho! viel Muth!

(Magdalene zieht Eva rasch durch die Vorhänge fort
Walther hat sich, aufgeregt und brütend, in einen erhöhten, kathederartigen Lehnstuhl geworfen, welchen zuvor
zwei Lehrbuben, von der Wand ab, mehr nach der Mitte
zu, gerückt hatten.

Noch mehrere Lehrbuben sind eingetreten: sie tragen
und richten Bänke, und bereiten Alles (nach der unten
folgenden Angabe) zur Sitzung der Meistersinger vor.)

Erster Lehrbube.
   David! was stehst?

Zweiter Lehrbube.   Greif's an's Werk!

Dritter Lehrbube.
   Hilf uns richten das Gemerk!

David.
   Zu eifrigst war ich vor euch allen:
   Nun schafft für euch; hab' ander Gefal-
   len!

Zweiter Lehrbube.
   Was der sich dünkt?

Dritter Lehrbube.   Der Lehrling Muster

Erster Lehrbube.
   Das macht, weil sein Meister ein Schuster.

Dritter Lehrbube.
   Beim Leisten sitzt er mit der Feder.

Zweiter Lehrbube.
   Beim Dichten mit Draht und Pfriem'.

Erster Lehrbube.
   Sein' Verse schreibt er auf rothes Leder.

Dritter Lehrbube.
(Mit der entsprechenden Gebärde.)
   Das, dächt' ich, gerbten wir ihm!
(Sie machen sich lachend an die fernere Herrichtung.)

David.
(Nachdem er den sinnenden Ritter eine Weile be-
trachtet, ruft sehr stark.)
   "Fanget an!"

Walter.

(Looking up, surprised.)
       What is it?

David.

(Still louder.)
" Now, begin ! " — So cries the Marker;
Then you must sing up; don't you know that?

Walter. Who is the Marker?

David.   Don't you know that?
T als of song were you never at?

Walter.
No, ne'er with for judge a trade-worker.

David. Are you a " Poet?"

Walter.   May be so!

David. Are you a " Singer?"

Walter.   I dont know.

David.
But " Schoolman," surely, and " Scholar "
  you've been?

Walter.
The terms I've never heard nor seen.

David.
And yet you would be at once a Master?

Walter.
Why should that seem to threaten disaster?

David. O Lena ! Lena !

Walter.   What do you say?

David. O Magdalena !

Walter.   Shew me the way !

David. The Tones and Modes we render
  Have many a form and name;
  The harsh ones and the tender:
  Who would try a list to frame?
A " Singer " and " Poet," both, d' ye see,
Previous to " Master " one must be

Walter. Who *is* a Poet?

Prentices.

(At work.)
      David ! ho there !

David. Presently, wait !
    (To Walter.)
      Who's Poet, sir?
When you a " Singer " have been created
And the Master-phrases have rightly stated,

Walther.

(Verwundert aufblickend.)
      Was soll's !

David.

(Noch stärker.)
" Fanget an ! " — So ruft der " Merker ;"
Nun sol t ihr singen : — wisst ihr das nicht?

Walther.
Wer ist der Merker?

David.   Wisst ihr das nicht.
War't ihr noch nie bei 'nem Sing-Gericht?

Walther.
Noch nie, wo die Richter Handwerker.

David.
Seid ihr ein " Dichter ? "

Walther.   Wär' ich's doch !

David.
Waret ihr " Singer ? "

Walther.   Wüsst ich's noch !

David.
Doch " Schulfreund " war't ihr, und " Schüler" zuvor?

Walther.
Das klingt mir alles fremd vor'm Ohr.

David.
Und so grad'hin wollt ihr Meister werden !

Walther.
Wie machte das so grosse Beschwerden?

David. O Lene ! O Lene !

Walther.   Wie ihr doch so thut!

David. O Magdalene !

Walther.   Rathet mir gut !

David. Der Meister Tön' und Weisen,
  Gar viel an Nam' und Zahl,
  Die starken und die leisen,
  Wer die wüsste allzumal !
Denn " Singer " und " Dichter " müsst ihr
  sein,
Eh' ihr zum " Meister " kehret ein.

Walther. Wer ist nun Dichter?

Lehrbuben.

(Während der Arbeit.)
      David ! kommst' her !

David. Warte nur, gleich ! —
    (Zu Walther.)
      Wer Dichter wär' ?
Habt ihr zum " Singer " euch aufgeschwun-
  gen
Und der Meister-Töne richtig gesungen,

If by yourself, with rhyme and word,
You can construct and let be heard
Straightway a novel Master-strain,
At once the Poet's prize you 'll gain.

Prentices.
Hey, David! shall we report this matter?
Will you never have finished your chatter?

David.
Oh, that 's it! When I 'm not by,
Of yourselves you place the things awry!

Walter.
Yet, one thing: Who is Master indeed?

David.
Sir knight, that matter is thus decreed:
The Poet who, with brain so witty,
To words and rhymes by himself prepared,
Can shape from the Tones a new Strain or
  Ditty,
He is a " Master-Singer " declared.

Walter.
          (Quickly.)
I only think of the Master-gain!
    If I sing,
    Vict'ry I wring
Only through verse with the proper strain.

David.
          (Turning to the Prentices.)
What are you doing? Because I'm not there,
All wrong you 're placing the platform and
  chair!
Is to-day " Song-class? " You know how;
Make smaller the stage! 'T is " Trial "
  now.

(The Prentices, who are preparing to erect a large platform hung with curtains in the middle of the stage, put this away, by David's direction, and build instead a smaller platform of boards; on this they place a seat with a little desk before it, near this a large black-board to which they hang a piece of chalk by a string; round this erection are hung black curtains, which are drawn round the back and sides and then over the front.)

Prentices.
          (During their work.)
Oh! of course, Master David is clev'rer than
  most!
Doubtless he 's hoping to get a high post.
      'T is Trial to-day,
      He 'll try away;
That he 's quite a " Singer " is now his boast.
The " Whack " rhyme he knows all through
  and through,
The " Sharp-hunger " tune he 'll sing you,
  too;

Füget ihr selbst nun Reim und Wort',
Dass sie genau an Stell' und Ort
Passten zu einem Meister-Ton,
Dann trüg't ihr den Dichterpreis davon.

Lehrbuben.
He, David! Soll man's dem Meister klagen!
Wirst dich bald des Schwatzens entschlagen?

David.
Oho! Ja wohl! Denn helf' ich euch nicht,
Ohne mich wird Alles doch falsch gericht'!

Walther.
Nun dies' noch; wer wird " Meister " genannt?

David.
Damit, Herr Ritter, ist's so bewandt! —
Der Dichter, der aus eig'nem Fleisse
Zu Wort' und Reimen, die er erfand,
Aus Tönen auch fügt eine neue Weise,
Der wird als " Meistersinger " erkannt.

Walther.
          (Rasch.)
So bleibt mir nichts als der Meisterlohn!
    Soll ich hier singen,
    Kann's nur gelingen,
Find' ich zum Vers auch den eig'nen Ton.

David.
          (Der sich zu den Lehrbuben gewendet.)
Was macht ihr denn da? — Ja, fehl' ich beim
  Werk,
Verkehrt nur richtet ihr Stuhl und Ge-
  merk! —
Ist denn heut' " Singschul'? " — dass ihr's
  wisst,
Das kleine Gemerk! — nur " Freiung " ist!

(Die Lehrbuben, welche Anstalt getroffen hatten, in der Mitte der Bühne ein grösseres Gerüste mit Vorhängen aufzuschlagen, schaffen auf Davids Weisung dies schnell bei Seite und stellen dafür ebenso eilig ein geringeres Brettbodengerüste auf; darauf stellen sie einen Stuhl mit einem kleinen Pult davor, daneben eine grosse schwarze Tafel, daran die Kreide am Faden aufgehängt wird; um das Gerüst sind schwarze Vorhänge angebracht, welche zunächst hinten und an beiden Seiten, dann auch vorn ganz zusammengezogen werden.)

Die Lehrbuben.
          (Während der Herrichtung.)
Aller End' ist doch David der Allerge-
  scheit'st!
Nach hohen Ehren gewiss er geizt:
      's ist Freiung heut';
      Gar sicher er freit,
Als vornehmer " Singer " schon er sich
  spreizt!
Die " Schlag "-Reime fest er inne hat,
" Arm-Hunger "-Weise singt er glatt;

But the "Hearty-kick" strain is what he
  knows best,
His master oft plays it him with zest.

        (They laugh.)

David.
  Aye, jeer away! but not at me;
  Another laughing-stock you'll see.
  He ne'er was "Scholar," learnt no singing,
  But yet o'er "Poets" would be springing;
      A noble knight he,
      In single fight he
  Thinks without any disaster
  Here to rise to a "Master."
      So settle with care
      Both stage and chair!
  Come here! Place there the board on wall,
  That on it the Marker's fingers may fall!
        (Turning to Walter.)
  Aye, Aye! the "Marker!" Are n't you
    afraid?
  With him have many their failures made.
  Seven faults you are suffered to make;
  They 're marked with his chalk ev 'ry one;
  If you commit one further mistake,
  You 're "outsung," and declared "outdone."
      So have a care!
      The Marker's there.
  God speed your Master-singing,
  May you the chaplet be winning;
  The wreath of flowers in silk so bright;
  I hope it may fall to your lot, sir knight!

The Prentices.
  (Who have closed the Marker's place, take hands and
dance in a ring round it.)

    "The wreath of flowers in silk so bright,
    I hope it may fall to your lot, sir knight."

(The erection is now completed in the following
manner:—at the R side covered benches are placed in
such a way as to curve towards the C. At the end of
these in the middle of the stage is the Marker's place, as
before described. L stands only the elevated seat ("the
Singer's Seat") opposite to the benches. At back, against
the large curtain, is a long, low bench for the Prentices—
Walter, vexed with the gibes of the boys, has seated himself on the front bench.

Pogner and Beckmesser enter from the sacristy, con-
versing; gradually the other masters assemble. The
Prentices, on seeing the Masters, enter, disperse and wait
respectfully by the back bench. Only David stands by
the entrance to the sacristy.)

Die "harte-Tritt"-Weis' doch kennt er am
  best',
Die trat ihm sein Meister hart und fest.
        (Sie lachen.)

David.
  Ja, lacht nur zu! Heut' bin ich's nicht;
  Ein Andrer stellt sich zum Gericht:
  Der war nicht "Schüler," ist nicht "Sin-
    ger,"
  Den "Dichter," sagt er, überspring' er;
      Denn er ist Junker,
      Und mit einem Sprung er
  Denkt ohne weit're Beschwerden
  Heut' hier "Meister" zu werden. —
      D'rum richtet nur fein
      Das Gemerk dem ein!
  Dorthin! — Hierher! — Die Tafel an die
    Wand,
  So dass sie recht dem Merker zur Hand!
        (Sich zu Walther umwendend.)
  Ja, ja! — dem "Merker!" — Wird euch wohl
    bang?
  Vor ihm schon mancher Werber vorsang.
  Sieben Fehler giebt er euch vor,
    Die merkt er mit Kreide dort an;
  Wer über sieben Fehler verlor,
    Hat versungen und ganz verthan!
      Nun nehmet euch in Acht!
      Der Merker wacht.
  Glück auf zum Meistersingen!
  Mög't ihr euch das Kränzlein erschwin-
    gen!
  Das Blumenkränzlein aus Seiden fein,
  Wird das dem Herrn Ritter beschieden
    sein?

Die Lehrbuben.
  (Welche das Gemerk zugleich geschlossen, fassen sich
an und tanzen einen verschlungenen Reihen darum.)

    "Das Blumenkränzlein aus Seiden fein
    Wird das dem Herrn Ritter beschieden
    sein?

(Die Einrichtung ist nun folgender Massen beendigt:—
Zur Seite rechts sind gepolsterte Bänke in der Weise
aufgestellt, dass sie einen schwachen Halbkreis nach der
Mitte zu bilden. Am Ende der Bänke, in der Mitte der
Scene, befindet sich das "Gemerk" benannte Gerüste,
welches zuvor hergerichtet worden. Zur linken Seite
rechts nur der erhöhte, kathedertige Stuhl ["der Singstuhl"] der Versammlung gegenüber. Im Hintergrunde,
den grossen Vorhang entlang, steht eine lange niedere
Bank für die Lehrlinge. Walther, verdriesslich über das
Gespött der Knaben, hat sich auf die vordere Bank niedergelassen.

Pogner und Beckmesser kommen im Gespräch aus der
Sacristei; allmählich versammeln sich immer mehrere der
Meister. Die Lehrbuben, als sie die Meister eintreten
sahen, sind sogleich zurückgegangen und harren ehrer-
bietig an der hinteren Bank. Nur David stellt sich
anfänglich am Eingang bei der Sacristei auf.)

Pogner.
(To Beckmesser.)
Trust me, my friendship is unshaken,
What I intend is for your good,
This trial must be undertaken;
None doubts your Mastership — who could?

Beckmesser.
But won't you in that matter falter,
Which caused in sooth my doubtful mood?
If Eva's whim the whole can alter,
What use is all my Masterhood?

Pogner.
Ah, what! It seems you've mainly rested
On that your hopes equivocal;
But if her heart's not interested,
How come you wooing her at all?

Beckmesser.
Why yes, that's true; therefore I drop a
Request that you will speak for me;
Say that my wooing's fair and proper,
That with Beckmesser you agree.

Pogner. With right good will

Beckmesser.
(Aside.)
He won't give way!
How shall I disappointment stay?

Walter.
(Who, on perceiving Pogner, has risen and advanced to meet him, now bows to him.)
Permit me, Master!

Pogner. What! Sir Walter?
(They greet one another.)

Beckmesser.
(Still to himself.)
If women had taste! But rather to palter
Than to hear poetry they prefer.

Walter.
This truly should be my proper groove.
I frankly state that what did move
Me from my land to part
Was solely love of Art.
I had forgotten to announce it,
But now in public I pronounce it:
A Master-Singer I would be.
Ope, Master, pray, the Guild to me.

(Other Masters have entered and advanced.)

Pogner.
(To those near him.)
Kunz Vogelgesang — Friend Nachtigal!

Pogner.
(Zu Beckmesser.)
Seid meiner Treue wohl versehen;
Was ich bestimmt, ist euch zu Nutz.
Im Wettgesang müsst ihr bestehen;
Wer böte euch als Meister Trutz?

Beckmesser.
Doch wollt ihr von dem Punkt nicht weichen,
Der mich — ich sag's — bedenklich macht;
Kann Evchen's Wunsch den Werber streichen,
Was nützt mir meine Meister-Pracht?

Pogner.
Ei, sagt! Ich mein', vor allen Dingen
Sollt' euch an dem gelegen sein?
Könnt ihr der Tochter Wunsch nicht zwingen,
Wie möchtet ihr wohl um sie frei'n?

Beckmesser.
Ei ja! Gar wohl! D'rum eben bitt' ich,
Dass bei dem Kind ihr für mich sprecht,
Wie ich geworben zart und sittig,
Und wie Beckmesser grad' euch recht.

Pogner. Das thu' ich gern.

Beckmesser.
(Bei Seite.)
Er lässt nicht nach!
Wie wehrt' ich da 'nem Ungemach?

Walther.
(Der, als er Pogner gewahrt, aufgestanden und ihm entgegengegangen ist, verneigt sich vor ihm.)
Gestattet, Meister!

Pogner. Wie! mein Junker!
Ihr sucht mich in der Singschul' hie?
(Sie begrüssen sich.)

Beckmesser.
(Immer bei Seite, für sich.)
Verstünden's die Frau'n! Doch schlechtes Geflunker
Gilt ihnen mehr als all' Poesie.

Walther.
Hie eben bin ich am rechten Ort
Gesteh' ich's frei, vom Lande fort,
Was mich nach Nürnberg trieb,
War nur zur Kunst die Lieb'.
Vergass ich's gestern euch zu sagen,
Heut' muss ich's laut zu künden wagen:
Ein Meistersinger möcht' ich sein.
Schliesst, Meister, in die Zunft mich ein!

(Andere Meister sind gekommen und herangetreten.)

Pogner.
(Zu den nächsten.)
Kunz Vogelgesang! Freund Nachtigall!

Hear what I've got to tell you all!
This noble knight, a friend of mine,
In the Master Art doth seek to shine.

(Greetings and introductions.)

Beckmesser.

(Still aside.)

Once more I 'll essay him, but if he 'll not waver
I 'll strive with my voice to win the maid's favor ;
In silent night, heard only by her.
I 'll see if my singing her heart can stir.
(Turns.)
What man is that?

Pogner.

(To Walter.)
'Faith, I am glad !
Old times are come again, my lad.

Beckmesser.

(Aside:)
I mislike his looks.

Pogner.

(Continuing.)
In your demand
My influence you may command.

Beckmesser.

(As before.)
What wants he here with his smiling air ?

Pogner.

(As before.)
Truly I helped you your lands to sell,
In our Guild I 'll enter you now as well.

Beckmesser.

(As before.)
Hallo, Sixtus !   Of him beware !

Walter.

(To Pogner.)
Best thanks I proffer
And gratitude offer !
Then have I permission
To seek for admission
As striver for the prize,
And Master-Singer to rise?

Beckmesser.
Oho ! that 's nice ! His ideas are not addled !

Pogner.
Sir Walter, these things with rules are saddled.
To-day is " Trial," I 'll state your case ;
The Masters will always lend me their face.

(The Master-Singers have now all assembled, Sachs the last.)

Sachs.   God greet ye, Masters !

Hört doch, welch' ganz besonderer Fall!
Der Ritter hier, mir wohlbekánnt,
Hat der Meisterkunst sich zugewandt.

(Begrüssungen.)

Beckmesser.

(Immer noch für sich.)

Noch such' ich's zu wenden: doch sollt' nicht gelingen,
Versuch' ich des Mädchens Herz zu ersingen·
In stiller Nacht, von ihr nur gehört,
Erfahr' ich, ob auf mein Lied sie schwört.
(Er wendet sich.)
Wer ist der Mensch?

Pogner.

(Zu Walther.)
Glaubt, wie mich's freut!
Die alte Zeit dünkt mich erneut.

Beckmesser.

(Immer noch für sich.)
Er gefällt mir nicht !

Pogner.

(Fortfahrend.)
Was ihr begehrt,
Soviel an mir, euch sei's gewährt.

Beckmesser.

(Ebenso.)
Was will der hier? — Wie der Blick ihm lacht !

Pogner.

(Ebenso.)
Half ich euch gern zu des Gut's Verkauf,
In die Zunft nun nehm' ich euch gleich gern auf.

Beckmesser.

(Ebenso.)
Holla ! Sixtus ! Auf den hab' Acht !

Walther.

(Zu Pogner.)
Habt Dank der Güte
Aus tiefstem Gemüthe !
Und darf ich denn hoffen,
Steht heut' mir noch offen
Zu werben um den Preis,
Dass ich Meistersinger heiss' ?

Beckmesser.
Oho ! Fein sacht ! Auf dem Kopf steht kein Kegel !

Pogner.
Herr Ritter, diess geh' nun nach der Regel
Doch heut' ist Freiung ! ich schlag' euch vor·
Mir leihen die Meister ein willig Ohr.

(Die Meistersinger sind nun alle angelangt, zuletzt auch Hans Sachs.)

Sachs.
Gott grüss' euch, Meister !

Vogelgesang. Are all arriven?

Beckmesser. Yes, Sachs is here, too.

Nachtigal. Let names be given.

Fritz Kothner.
(Produces a list, stands apart from the rest, and calls.)
　　To hold a Trial-examination,
　　Masters, I give ye invitation;
　　　　Of one and all
　　　　The names I call,
　　And first my own, which though I note ne'er,
　　I answer to, and am Fritz Kothner.
　　Are you there, Veit Pogner?

Pogner. Here at hand.
　　　　　　(Sits.)

Kothner. Kunz Vogelgesang?

Vogelgesang. Yes, here I stand.
　　　　　　(Sits.)

Kothner. Herman Ortel?

Ortel. Comes when he ought.
　　　　　　(Sits.)

Kothner. Balthazar Zorn?

Zorn. Ne'er late I'm caught.
　　　　　　(Sits.)

Kothner. Conrad Nachtigal

Nachtigal. True as my song.
　　　　　　(Sits.)

Kothner. Augustin Moser?

Moser. Here all along.
　　　　　　(Sits.)

Kothner. Nicholas Vogel? — No?

A Prentice.
　　(Jumping up from his seat at back.)
　　　　　　He's ill.

Kothner. God send him recovery.

All the Masters. Amen.

Prentice. Good will.
　　　　(Sits down again.)

Kothner. Hans Sachs?

David.
　　(Officiously rising.)
　　　　　　He's there, sir.

Sachs.
　　(Threatening David.)
　　　　　　Tingles thy skin?—
　　Excuse me, Master! Sachs has come in.
　　　　(Sits.)

Kothner. Sixtus Beckmesser?

Vogelgesang. Sind wir beisammen?

Beckmesser.
　　Der Sachs ist ja da!

Nachtigall. So ruft die Namen.

Fritz Kothner.
(Zieht eine Liste hervor, stellt sich zur Seite auf und ruft.)
　　Zu einer Freiung und Zunftberathung
　　Ging an die Meister ein' Einladung:
　　　　Bei Nenn' und Nam'
　　　　Ob jeder kam,
　　Ruf' ich nun auf, als letzt-entbot'ner,
　　Der ich mich nenn' und bin Fritz Kothner.
　　Seid ihr da, Veit Pogner?

Pogner. Hier zur Hand.
　　　　(Er setzt sich.)

Kothner. Kunz Vogelgesang?

Vogelgesang. Ein sich fand.
　　　　(Setzt sich.)

Kothner. Hermann Ortel?

Ortel. Immer am Ort.
　　　　(Setzt sich.)

Kothner. Balthasar Zorn?

Zorn. Bleibt niemals fort.
　　　　(Setzt sich.)

Kothner. Konrad Nachtigall?

Nachtigall. Treu seinem Schlag.
　　　　(Setzt sich.)

Kothner. Augustin Moser?

Moser. Nie fehlen mag.
　　　　(Setzt sich.)

Kothner. Niklaus Vogel? — Schweigt?

Ein Lehrbube.
　　(Sich schnell von der Bank erhebend.)
　　　　　　Ist krank.

Kothner. Gut' Bess'rung dem Meister!

Alle Meister. Walt's Gott!

Der Lehrbube. Schön Dank!
　　　　(Setz sich wieder.)

Kothner. Hans Sachs?

David.
　　(Vorlaut sich erhebend.)
　　　　　　Da steht er!

Sachs.
　　(Drohend zu David.)
　　　　　　Juckt dich das Fell? —
　　Verzeiht, Meister! — Sachs ist zur Stell'.
　　　　(Er setz sich.)

Kothner. Sixtus Beckmesser?

Beckmesser.   Always near Sachs,
Then I have a rhyme to " bloom and wax."
   (Sits close to Sachs, who laughs.)

Kothner. Ulrich Eisslinger?

Eisslinger.   Here!
     (Sits.)

Kothner.   Hans Foltz?

Foltz. I'm there.
    (Sits.)

Kothner. Hans Schwarz?

Schwarz.   The list now halts.
     (Sits.)

Kothner. The meeting's full; a goodly show.
Shall we make choice of a Marker now?

Vogelgesang. The festival first.

Beckmesser.
   (To Kothner.)
     If you are pressed,
My turn I'll yield to you with zest.

Pogner.
 Not yet, my Masters! let that alone,
A weighty matter I would make known.
 (All the Masters rise and reseat themselves.)

Kothner. With pleasure, Master; tell.

Beckmesser.   Immer bei Sachs,
Dass den Reim ich lern' von "blüh' und
wachs'."
  (Er setzt sich neben Sachs, dieser lacht.)

Kothner. Ulrich Eisslinger?

Eisslinger.   Hier!
   (Setzt sich.)

Kothner.   Hans Foltz?

Foltz. Bin da.
   (Setzt sich.)

Kothner. Hans Schwarz?

Schwarz.   Zuletzt: Gott wollt's!
   (Setzt sich.)

Kothner. Zur Sitzung gut und voll die Zahl.
Beliebt's, wir schreiten zur Merkerwahl?

Vogelgesang. Wohl eh'r nach dem Fest.

Beckmesser.
   (Zu Kothner.)
     Pressirt's den Herrn?
Mein Stell' und Amt lass' ich ihm gern.

Pogner.
 Nicht doch, ihr Meister! Lasst das jetzt fort.
Für wicht'gen Antrag bitt' ich um's Wort.
 (Alle Meister stehen auf und setzen sich wieder.)

Kothner.
Das habt ihr, Meister! Sprecht!

FOGNER'S ADDRESS.

(POGNER'S ANREDE.)

English Version by L. U.

Moderato. POGNER.

Give heed now to what I say!
Nun hört, und ver-steht mich recht!
The feast of John the Bap-tist's
Das schö-ne Fest, Jo-han-nis-

day You know we keep to-mor-row:
tag, ihr wisst begeh'n wir mor-gen:
On mea-dow green, 'mid flow-ers gay, With feast, and
auf grü-ner Au', am Blu-men-hag, bei Spiel und

dance, and mer-ry play, The cares the mind be-set-ting With mer-ry heart for-
Tanz im Lust-ge-lag, an fro-her Brust ge-bor-gen, ver-ges-sen sei-ner

get-ting, Each one re-joic-es as he may. The sing-ing school to great church
Sor-gen, ein Je-der freut sich, wie er mag. Die Sing-schul' ernst im Kir-chen

no - tion. Yet how this to our hon - or stands, That no - bly, as man should, We
le - gen. Doch wie uns das zur Eh - re ge - reich', und das mit ho - hem Muth wir

prize the fair and good, That art . . in ev - 'ry form we love, 'Twas this to the world I
schä - tzen was schön und gut, was werth die Kunst und was sie gilt, das ward ich der Welt zu

wish'd to prove, And there - fore, mas - ters, know What gift I shall be - stow!
zei - gen ge - willt, d'rum hört, Meis - ter die Gab' die als Preis be - stimmt ich hab'!

The vic - - tor in the art of song, Who wins the prize be - fore the throng,
Dem Sie - - ger der im Kunst - ge - sang vor al - lem Volk den Preis er - rang,

On John the Bap - tist's day, Be he who - e'er he may, Him give I, of art a
am Sanct Jo - han - nis - tag, sei er, wer er auch mag, dem geb ich, ein Kunst - ge -

lov - er, Of Nu - rem - berg, Veit Pog - ner, With gold and
wog - ner, von Nü - ren - berg Veit Pog - ner, mit all' mein - em

lands and all be - side, E - va, my on - ly child, as bride!
Gut, wie's geh' und steh', E - va, mein ein - zig Kind, zur Eh'!

The Masters.	**Die Meister.**
(Animatedly to one another.)	*(Sehr lebhaft durcheinander.)*
That's nobly said! Brave words — brave man!	Das nenn' ich ein Wort! Ein Wort, ein Mann!
You see now what a Nuremberger can!	Da sieht man, was ein Nürnberger kann!
So far and wide we 'll raise always	D'rob preis't man euch noch weit und breit,
The worthy burgher Pogner's praise!	Den wack'ren Bürger Pogner Veit!
Prentices.	**Die Lehrbuben.**
(Jumping up merrily.)	*(Lustig aufspringend.)*
All our days raise and blaze	Alle Zeit, weit und breit,
Pogner's praise.	Pogner Veit!
Vogelgesang.	**Vogelgesang.**
Who would not now unmarried be!	Wer möchte da nicht ledig' sein!
Sachs.	**Sachs.**
There 's some would give their wives with glee.	Sein Weib' gäb' gern wohl mancher d'rein!
Nachtigal. Come, single man,	**Nachtigall.**
Do all ye can.	Auf, ledig' Mann!
	Jetzt macht euch dran!
Pogner. My meaning you must clearly see;	**Pogner.**
No lifeless gift I offer you;	Nun hört noch, wie ich's ernstlich mein'!
	Ein' leblos' Gabe stell' ich nicht:

The maid shall sit in judgment, too.
Our Guild the winner shall declare,
But as to marriage, 't is but fair
    That, 'spite the Master's choice,
    The bride should have a voice.

Beckmesser.
                    (To Kothner.)
Do you like that?

Kothner.
                    (Aloud.)
                    You mean to say
That we the maiden must obey.

Beckmesser.   'T were dangerous!

Kothner.   I cannot see
How then our judgment would be free.

Beckmesser.
Let her choose as may please her heart,
And leave the Master-Song business apart.

Pogner.   Nay, nay! why so? Let me correct!
Any man whom we all elect
    May be by her rejected,
    But never another accepted:
A Master-Singer he must be;
None may she wed uncrowned by ye.

Sachs.   But stay!
Perhaps that were too much to say.
The fire that warms a maiden's heart
Is not like flames of Master-Art;
Undisciplined, the female mind
Level with public voice I find.
So, if you hold to public vision
    Your high esteem of Art,
If you desire the girl's decision
    Should not the matter thwart,
Then let the people, too, decide;
With the maiden's voice they 'd coincide.
        (The Prentices jump up and rub their hands.)

Beckmesser.   Hey! Are not the boys contented!

Sachs.
                    (Earnestly continuing.)
So may it be ne'er repented
That once, on St. John's day, ev'ry year,
Ye do not bring the people here,
But bend your Guild of Masters proud
Right willingly towards the crowd.
    You cater here for the masses;
    I think then 't were but right
    To ask the vote of those classes
    And hear if they find delight.

Ein Mägdlein sitzt mit zu Gericht.
Den Preis erkennt die Meister-Zunft;
Doch gilt's der Eh', so will's Vernunft,
    Dass ob der Meister Rath
    Die Braut den Ausschlag hat.

Beckmesser.
                    (Zu Kothner.)
Dünkt euch das klug?

Kothner.
                    (Laut.)
                    Versteh' ich gut,
Ihr gebt uns in des Mägdlein's Huth?

Beckmesser.
Gefährlich das!

Kothner.   Stimmt es nicht bei.
Wie wäre dann der Meister Urtheil frei?

Beckmesser.
Lasst's gleich wählen nach Herzen's Ziel,
Und lasst den Meistergesang aus dem Spiel.

Pogner.
Nicht so! Wie doch! Versteht mich recht!
Wenn ihr Meister den Preis zusprecht,
    Die Maid kann dem verwehren,
    Doch nie einen Andren begehren:
Ein Meistersinger muss er sein;
Nur wen ihr krönt, den soll sie frei'n.

Sachs.   Verzeiht!
Vielleicht schon ginget ihr zu weit.
Ein Mädchenherz und Meisterkunst
Erglüh'n nicht stets von gleicher Brunst;
Der Frauen Sinn, gar unbelehrt,
Dünkt mich dem Sinn des Volks gleich
    werth.
Wollt ihr nun vor dem Volke zeigen,
    Wie hoch die Kunst ihr ehrt;
Und lasst ihr dem Kind die Wahl zu eigen,
    Wollt nicht, dass dem Spruch es
    wehrt':
So lasst das Volk auch Richter sein;
Mit dem Kinde sicher stimmts überein,
(Die Lehrbuben springen auf und reiben sich die
Hände.)

Beckmesser.
Hei! wie sich die Buben freuen!

Sachs.
                    (Eifrig fortfahrend.)
                    D'rum möcht's euch nie gereuen,
Dass jährlich am Sankt Johannisfest,
Statt dass das Volk man kommen lässt,
Herab aus hoher Meister-Wolk'
Ihr selbst euch wendet zu dem Volk'.
    Dem Volke wollt ihr behagen;
    Nun dächt' ich, läg es nah',
    Ihr liesset es selbst euch auch sagen,
    Ob das ihm zur Last geschah?

Thus Art and Nation shall bloom and wax
By your good help, say I, Hans Sachs.

Vogelgesang.   That's very right!

Kothner.   And yet all wrong!

Nachtigal.
  When riff-raff speak I'll hold my tongue.

Kothner.
  Our Art would quickly be disgraced,
  If it were swayed by public taste.

Beckmesser.
  He's tried for that who talks so loud;
  Clap-trap stuff he writes for the crowd.

Pogner.   Friend Sachs, what I propose is new;
  Too many novelties won't do!—
  I ask, then, if ye Masters will hold
  My offer on the terms just told?
        (The Masters rise assentingly.)

Sachs.   I am content the maid should decide.

Beckmesser.
                (Aside.)
  That cobbler-man I can't abide!

Kothner.   What candidate comes to me?
  A bachelor he must be.

Beckmesser.
  He may be a widower!   How about Sachs?

Sachs.
  Nay, nay, good Marker!   Of younger wax
  Must be the suitor who comes to woo
  Our Eva, than myself or you.

Beckmesser.   Than even I?—Mannerless
  knave!

Kothner.   If suitors offer, their names I crave!
  Is any one here who seeks to essay?

Pogner.
  Well, Masters, to the work of the day!
      And be it understood
  That I, as Masters should,
      To this knight have offered protection,
      Who seeks for our election
  To woo, as Master-Singers may.—
  Sir Walter von Stolzing step this way!
      (Walter advances and makes obeisance.)
  Sir Walter Stolzing, Franconian knight:
  My friends his praise both speak and write,
  The last survivor of his race,
  He lately left his native place

Dass Volk und Kunst gleich blüh' und
  wachs',
Bestellt ihr so, mein' ich Hans Sachs.

Vogelgesang.   Ihr meint's wohl recht!

Kothner.   Doch steht's d'rum faul.

Nachtigall.
  Wenn spricht das Volk, halt' ich das Maul.

Kothner.
  Der Kunst droht' allweil' Fall und Schmach,
  Läuft sie der Gunst des Volkes nach.

Beckmesser.
  D'rin bracht' er's weit, der hier so dreist:
  Gassenhauer dichtet er meist.

Pogner.
  Freund Sachs, was ich mein', ist schon neu:
  Zuviel auf einmal brächte Reu'!—
  So frag' ich, ob den Meistern gefällt,
  Gab' und Regel, wie ich's gestellt?
        (Die Meister erheben sich.)

Sachs.
  Mir genügt der Jungfer Ausschlag-Stimm'.

Beckmesser.
                (Für sich.)
  Der Schuster weckt doch stets mir Grimm!

Kothner.   Wer schreibt sich als Werber ein?
      Ein Jung-Gesell muss es sein.

Beckmesser.
  Vielleicht auch ein Wittwer?   Fragt nur den
  Sachs!

Sachs.
  Nicht doch, Herr Merker!   Aus jüng'rem
  Wachs
  Als ich und ihr muss der Freier sein,
  Soll Evchen ihm den Preis verleih'n.

Beckmesser.
  Als wie auch ich?—Grober Gesell!

Kothner.
  Begehrt wer Freiung, der komm' zur Stell'!
  Ist Jemand gemeld't der Freiung begehrt!

Pogner.
  Wohl Meister! Zur Tagesordnung kehrt!
      Und nehmt von mir Bericht,
      Wie ich auf Meister-Pflicht
      Einen jungen Ritter empfehle,
      Der wünscht, dass man ihn wähle,
  Und heut' als Meistersinger frei'.—
  Mein Junker von Stolzing, kommt herbei!
        (Walter tritt vor und verneigt sich.)
  Von Stolzing Walther aus Frankenland,
  Nach Brief' und Urkund mir wohlbekannt.
  Als seines Stammes letzter Spross,
  Verliess er neulich Hof und Schloss,

To Nuremberg to come
And make this town his home.

Beckmesser.
(To his neighbor.)
Young good-for-nothing! This is nice!

Nachtigal.
(Aloud.)
Friend Pogner's word will quite suffice.

Sachs. We Masters did long since decide
Nor lord nor peasant should be denied.
Art is indeed the sole concern
Of those who Master-Song would learn.

Kothner. First I pray you impart
What Master taught you your Art.

Walter. By silent hearth in winter tide,
When house and hall in snow did hide,
How once the Spring so sweetly smiled
And soon should wake to glory mild,
An ancient book my sire compiled
Set all before me duly:
Sir Walter von der Vogelweid'
Has been my master, truly.

Sachs. A goodly master!

Beckmesser. But long since dead!
So what could he of our precepts have read?

Kothner. But in any school or college
Of singing gained you your knowledge?

Walter. Yes, when the fields the frost defied
Beneath returning summer-tide,
What once in dreary winter's night
Within that book I read aright
Now pealed aloud through forest bright:
I heard the music ringing.
The wood before the Vogelweid'—
'T was there I learnt my singing.

Beckmesser. Can any one his meaning trace?

Vogelgesang. Good sooth, he's bold!

Nachtigal. Peculiar case!

Kothner. Now, Masters, if you will,
The Marker's place we'll fill.
Sacred theme do you choose, sir knight?

Walter. My sacred trove's
The banner of love,
Swung and sung to my delight!

Kothner. Secular be it. Now inside,
Marker Beckmesser, please to hide.

Und zog nach Nürnberg her,
Dass er hier Bürger wär'.

Beckmesser.
(Zum Nachbar.)
Neu Junker-Unkraut! Thut nicht gut.

Nachtigall.
(Laut.)
Freund Pogner's Wort Genüge thut.

Sachs.
Wie längst von den Meistern beschlossen ist,
Ob Herr, ob Bauer, hier nichts beschliesst:
Hier fragt sich's nach der Kunst allein,
Wer will ein Meistersinger sein.

Kothner. D'rum nun frag' ich zur Stell':
Welch' Meister's seid ihr Gesell'?

Walther. Am stillen Herd in Winterszeit,
Wenn Burg und Hof mir eingeschnei't,
Wie einst der Lenz so lieblich lacht',
Und wie er bald wohl neu erwacht',
Ein altes Buch, vom Ahn' vermacht'
Gab das mir oft zu lesen:
Herr Walther vor. der Vogelweid',
Der ist mein Meister gewesen.

Sachs. Ein guter Meister!

Beckmesser. Doch lang schon todt·
Wie lehrt' ihm der wohl der Regel Gebot?

Kothner. Doch in welcher Schul' das Singen
Mocht' euch zu lernen gelingen?

Walther.
Wann dann die Flur vom Frost befreit,
Und wiederkehrt die Sommerszeit,
Was einst in langer Winternacht
Das alte Buch mir kund gemacht,
Das schallte laut in Waldespracht,
Das hört' ich hell erklingen:
Im Wald dort auf der Vogelweid'
Da lernt' ich auch das Singen.

Beckmesser.
Entnahmt ihr was der Worte Schwall?

Vogelgesang. Ei nun, er wagt's.

Nachtigall. Merkwürd'ger Fall!

Kothner. Nun Meister, wenn's gefällt,
Werd' das Gemerk bestellt.—
Wählt der Herr einen heil'gen Stoff!

Walther. Was heilig mir,
Der Liebe Panier,
Schwing' und sing' ich, mir zu Hoff'.

Kothner.
Das gilt uns weltlich. D'rum allein,
Merker Beckmesser, schliesst euch ein!

Beckmesser.
(Rising and going as if reluctantly to the Marker's box.
  Unpleasant work, and more so now ;
  My chalk will harass you, I trow !
          Sir knight, now hark !
  Sixtus Beckmesser goes to mark.
          Here in this cell
  He silently does his duty fell.
  Seven faults are given you clear ;
          With chalk on a slate they are scored :
  But if more mistakes than seven appear,
          Then, sir knight, without hope you are
          floor'd.
          My ears are keen ;
  But as, if what I do were seen,
          You might be curbed,
          Be not disturbed ;
          I hide myself from view : —
          So Heav'n be kind to you.
(He has seated himself in the box and with the last
words stretches his head out with a scornfully familiar
nod, then pulls to the front curtains, which a Prentice had
opened for him, so that he becomes invisible.)

Kothner.
(Taking down the " *Leges Tabulaturae* " which the
Prentices had hung upon the wall.)
  All that belongs to song mature
  Now hear read from the Tabulature.
          (Reads.)
  " Each Master-Singer-created Stave
  Its regular measurement must have,
  By sundry regulations stated
  And never violated.
  What we call a ' Section' is two Stanzas ;
  For each the self-same melody answers :
  A Stanza several lines doth blend,
  And each line with a rhyme must end.
  Then come we to the ' After-Song,'
  Which must be also some lines long,
  And have its especial melody
  Which from the other must diff'rent be.
  So Staves and Sections of such measure
  A Master-Song may have at pleasure.
  He who a new song can outpour,
  Which in four syllables — not more —
  Another strain doth plagiarize,
  He may obtain the Master-Prize." —
  Now sit you on the Singer's stool !

Walter.   Here, on this stool ?

Kothner.   It is the rule.

Walter.
          (Mounting the stool, with dissatisfaction.)
  For thee I 'm sitting, love, herein.

Kothner.
          (Loudly.)
  The Singer sits !

Beckmesser.
          (Aufstehend und dem Gemerk zuschreitend.)
  Ein sau'res Amt, und heut' zumal ;
  Wohl giebt's mit der Kreide manche Qual.
          Herr Ritter wisst :
  Sixtus Beckmesser Merker ist ;
          Hier im Gemerk
  Verrichtet er sein strenges Werk.
  Sieben Fehler giebt er euch vor,
          Die merkt er mit der Kreide dort an ;
  Wenn er über sieben Fehler verlor,
          Dann versang er Herr Rittersmann.
          Gar fein er hört :
  Doch dass er euch den Muth nicht stört,
          Säh't ihr ihm zu,
          So giebt er euch Ruh',
          Und schliesst sich gar hier ein, —
          Lässt Gott euch befohlen sein.
(Er hat sich in das Gemerk gesetzt, streckt mit dem
Letzten den Kopf höhnisch freundlich nickend heraus, und
zieht den vorderen Vorhang, den zuvor einer der Lehrbu-
ben geöffnet hatte, wieder ganz zusammen, so dass er un
sichtbar wird.)

Kothner.
(Hat die von den Lehrbuben aufgehängten " *Leges Ta-
bulaturae* " von der Wand genommen.)
  Was euch zum Leide Richt' und Schnur,
  Vernehmt nun aus der Tabulatur. —
          (Er liest.)
  " Ein jedes Meistersanges Bar
  Stell' ordentlich ein Gemässe dar
  Aus unterschiedlichen Gesetzen,
  Die Keiner soll verletzen.
  Ein Gesetz besteht aus zweenen Stollen,
  Die gleiche Melodei haben sollen ;
  Der Stoll' aus etlicher Vers' Gebänd',
  Der Vers hat seinen Reim am End'.
  Darauf so folgt der Abgesang,
  Der sei auch etlich' Verse lang,
  Und hab' sein' besondere Melodei,
  Als nicht im Stollen zu finden sei.
  Derlei Gemässes mehre Baren
  Soll ein jed' Meisterlied bewahren ;
  Und wer ein neues Lied gericht',
  Das über vier der Sylben nicht
  Eingreift in andrer Meister Weis',
  Des' Lied erwerb' sich Meister-Preis." —
  Nun setzt euch in den Singstuhl !

Walther.
  Hier in den Stuhl ?

Kothner.   Wie's Brauch der Schul'

Walther.
(Besteigt den Stuhl und setzt sich mit Missbehagen.)
  Für dich, Geliebte, sei's gethan !

Kothner.
          (Sehr laut.)
  Der Sänger sitzt.

Beckmesser.
(From his box, very harshly.)
Now begin!

Walter.
(After a short consideration.)
Now begin!—
So cries through woodlands the Spring,
And makes them loudly ring:
Then, as to distance urging,
The echoes ripple thence,
From far there comes a surging
That swells with pow'r intense:
It booms and bounds,
The forest sounds
With thousand heavenly voices;
Now loud and clear,
Approaching near,
The murmurs steal
Like bells that peal
Exultant Nature rejoices!
This call,
How all
The wood an answer makes,
As life again awakes,
Pouring forth
A tender song of Spring!

(During this, repeated groans of discouragement and scratchings of the chalk are heard from the Marker. Walter hears them also, and after a momentary pause of discomposure continues.)

There, like a hiding craven
With hate and envy torn,
A thorny hedge his haven,
Sits Winter, all forlorn,
In withered leaves array'd
His lurking head is laid;
He seeks the joyous singing
To sorrow to be bringing.
(Rising from the stool in displeasure.)
But — "Now begin!"
So cried a voice in my breast
Ere aught of love I had guess'd;
There stirred a deep emotion
And waked me, as I had slept:
My heart with throbbing commotion
My bosom's restraint o'erlept:
My blood did course
With giant force,
To novel sensations soaring;
From warmth of night
With boundless might
Sighs hurried me
Towards the sea,
The pent-up passion outpouring:
The call
How all

Beckmesser.
(Im Gemerk, sehr grell.)
Fanget an!

Walther.
(Nach einiger Sammlung.)
Fanget an!
So rief der Lenz in den Wald,
Dass laut es ihn durchhallt:
Und wie in fern'ren Wellen
Der Hall von dannen flieht,
Von weither nah't ein Schwellen,
Das mächtig näher zieht;
Es schwillt und schallt,
Es tönt der Wald
Von holder Stimmen Gemenge;
Nun laut und hell
Schon nah' zur Stell',
Wie wächst der Schwall!
Wie Glockenhall
Ertos't des Jubels Gedränge!
Der Wald,
Wie bald
Antwortet' er dem Ruf,
Der neu ihm Leben schuf,
Stimmte an
Das süsse Lenzes-Lied!—

(Man hat aus dem Gemerk wiederholt unmuthige Seufzer des Merkers, und heftiges Anstreichen mit der Kreide vernommen. Auch Walther hat es bemerkt, und fährt dadurch für eine kurze Weile gestört, fort.)

In einer Dornenhecken,
Von Neid und Gram verzehrt,
Musst' er sich da verstecken,
Der Winter, Grimm-bewehrt:
Von dürrem Laub umrauscht
Er lauert da und lauscht,
Wie er das frohe Singen
Zu Schaden könnte bringen.—
(Unmuthig vom Stuhl aufstehend.)
Doch: fanget an!
So rief es mir in die Brust,
Als ich noch von Liebe nicht wusst'.
Da fühlt' ich's tief sich regen,
Als weckt' es mich aus dem Traum;
Mein Herz mit bebenden Schlägen
Erfüllte des Busen's Raum:
Das Blut, es wall't
Mit Allgewalt,
Geschwellt von neuem Gefühle;
Aus warmer Nacht
Mit Uebermacht
Schwillt mir zum Meer
Der Seufzer Heer
In wildem Wonne-Gewühle:
Die Brust
Mit Lust

My breast an answer makes,
As life anew it takes,
    Pouring forth
A glorious lay of love!

Beckmesser.
(Who has grown still more restive, tears open the curtains.)
  Is 't nearly finished?

Walter.   What means this call?

Beckmesser.
(Holding out the slate completely covered with chalk-marks.)
  I've finished with the slate, that 's all!
    (The Masters cannot restrain their laughter.)

Walter. Yet hear! My lady's praise to ring,
My second verse I ought to sing.

Beckmesser.
        (Leaving his box.)
  Sing where you will! Here you 're undone.
My Masters, see the slate, ev'ry one:
The like of this I never knew;
I'd credit no man's work thereto!
    (The Masters are in commotion.)
Walter. D' ye let him, Masters, plague me so!
Shall I be heard by you or no?

Pogner.
  One word, friend Marker! You 're somewhat
    wroth?

Beckmesser.
  Be Marker he who likes henceforth!
But that this man is quite out-sung
You can decide yourselves among.

Sachs.
(Who has listened to Walter from the first with serious interest.)
  Not all have like opinion passed.
    The song you 've so derided
  To me is new, but not confused:
    Though not by us 't was guided,
  His course was firm, as though well used.
    One way you measure solely
  A work that your rules do not fit:
    Resign your own views wholly,
  Some other rules apply to it.

Beckmesser.
  Aha! That 's fine! Just listen, pray!
Sachs opes a gap for fools that way,
    Where in and out at pleasure
    Their minds a course can measure.
Let in the streets the rabble holloa;
Here must we, at least, some discipline
  follow.

Antwortet sie dem Ruf,
Der neu ihr Leben schuf:
    Stimmt nun an
Das hehre Liebes-Lied!

Beckmesser.
(Der immer unruhiger geworden, reisst den Vorhang auf.)
  Seid ihr nun fertig?

Walther.   Wie fraget ihr?
Beckmesser.
(Die ganz mit Kreidestrichen bedeckte Tafel heraus-haltend.)
  Mit der Tafel ward ich fertig schier.
    (Die Meister müssen lachen.)

Walther.
  Hört doch! Zu meiner Frauen Preis
Gelang' ich jetzt erst mit der Weis'.

Beckmesser.
      (Das Gemerk verlassend.)
  Singt, wo ihr wollt! Hier habt ihr ver-
  than.—
Ihr Meister, schaut die Tafel euch an:
So lang ich leb', ward's nicht erhört;
Ich glaubt's nicht, wenn ihr's all' auch
  schwört!
    (Die Meister sind im Aufstand durcheinander.)

Walther.
  Erlaubt ihr's, Meister, dass er mich stört?
Blieb' ich von Allen ungehört?

Pogner.
  Ein Wort, Herr Merker! Ihr seid gereizt?

Beckmesser.
  Sei Merker fortan, wer darnach geizt!
Doch dass der Ritter versungen hat,
Beleg' ich erst noch vor der Meister Rath.

Sachs.
(Der vom Beginn an Walther mit zunehmendem Ernst zugehört hat.)
  Nicht jeder eure Meinung theilt.—
    Des Ritters Lied und Weise,
  Sie fand ich neu, doch nicht verwirrt;
    Verliess er uns're G'leise,
  Schritt er doch fest und unbeirrt.
    Wollt ihr nach Regeln messen,
  Was nicht nach eurer Regeln Lauf,
    Der eig'nen Spur vergessen,
  Sucht davon erst die Regeln auf!

Beckmesser.
  Aha! Schon recht! Nun hört ihr's doch,
Den Stümpern öffnet Sachs ein Loch,
    Da aus und ein nach Belieben
    Ihr Wesen leicht sie trieben.
Singet dem Volk auf Markt und Gassen:
Hier wird nach den Regeln nur eingelassen

Sachs. Friend Marker, why in such a flutter?
　　Wherefore so angry, pray?
　A riper judgment you might utter,
　　If better heed you'd pay.
　And so, to speak my final word,
　The young knight to the end must be heard.

Beckmesser.
　The Master's Guild, the school and all,
　Weighed against Sachs' word must fall.

Sachs. The Lord forbid I should demand
　Aught contrary to our law's command:
　　But surely there 't is written:
　" The Marker shall be chosen so,
　　By prejudice unbitten
　That nought of bias he may show."
　If this one turns his step to wooing
　Can he refrain a wrong from doing,
　To bring to shame 'fore all the school,
　His rival yonder on the stool?
　　　　　(Walter flames up.)

Nachtigal. You go too far!

Kothner. Too free you are!

Pogner.
　　　　(To the Masters.)
　I pray you, Masters, cease this jar.

Beckmesser.
　Hey! What needs Master Sachs to mention
　　Which way my steps may be turned?
　With the state of my *sole* his attention
　　Better might be concerned!
　But since my shoemaker follows the Muse
　It fares but ill with my boots and shoes.
　　　Just look, how they're split!
　　　See, here's a great slit!
　　All of his verse and rhyme
　　I would declare sublime;
　His dramas, plays, his farces and all,
　If with my new pair of shoes he'd call.

Sachs.
　　　(Scratching his head.)
　　I fear you have me there:
　　But, Master, if 't is fair
　That on the merest boor's shoe-leather
　　Some little verse I frame,
　I ask you, worthy town-clerk, whether
　　You should not have the same?
　A motto such as you require,
　With all my poor poetic fire
　　Not yet I've hit upon;
　　But I will come anon,
　When I have heard the knight's song through:
　So let him sing on without ado!
　　(Walter, much put out, remounts the Singer's Seat.)

The Masters. Enough! Conclude!

Sachs.
　Herr Merker, was doch solch ein Eifer?
　　Was doch so wenig Ruh'?
　Eu'r Urtheil, dünkt mich, wäre reifer,
　　Hörtet ihr besser zu.
　Darum, so komm ich jetzt zum Schluss,
　Dass den Junker zu End' man hören muss.

Beckmesser.
　Der Meister Zunft, die ganze Schul',
　Gegen den Sachs da sind wie Null.

Sachs. Verhüt' es Gott, was ich begehr',
　Dass das nicht nach den Gesetzen wär'!
　　Doch da nun steht's geschrieben,
　Der Merker werde so bestellt,
　　Dass weder Hass noch Lieben
　Das Urtheil trüben, das er fällt,
　Geht er nun gar auf Freiers-Füssen,
　Wie sollt' er da die Lust nicht büssen
　Den Nebenbuhler auf dem Stuhl
　Zu schmähen vor der ganzen Schul'!
　　　　(Walther flammt auf.)

Nachtigall. Ihr geht zu weit!

Kothner. Persönlichkeit!

Pogner.
　　　(Zu den Meistern.)
　Vermeidet, Meister, Zwist und Streit!

Beckmesser.
　Ei, was kümmert's doch Meister Sachsen,
　　Auf was für Füssen ich geh'?
　Liess' er d'rob lieber Sorge sich wachsen,
　　Dass nichts mir drück' die Zeh'!
　Doch seit mein Schuster ein grosser Poet,
　Gar übel es um mein Schuhwerk steht!
　　　Da seht, wie es schlappt,
　　　Und überall klappt!
　　All' seine Vers' und Reim'
　　Liess' ich ihm gern daheim,
　Historien, Spiel' und Schwänke dazu,
　Brächt' er mir morgen die neuen Schuh'!

Sachs. Ihr mahnt mich da gar recht:
　　Doch schickt sich's, Meister, sprecht,
　Dass, find' ich selbst dem Eseltreiber
　　Ein Sprüchlein auf die Sohl',
　Dem hochgelahrten Herrn Stadtschreiber
　　Ich nichts d'rauf schreiben soll?
　Das Sprüchlein, das eu'r würdig sei,
　Mit all' meiner armen Poeterei
　　Fand ich noch nicht zur Stund';
　　Doch wird's wohl jetzt mir kund,
　Wenn ich des Ritters Lied gehört:—
　D'rum sing er nun weiter ungestört!
　(Walther, in grosser Aufregung, stellt sich auf den Sing stuhl.)

Die Meister. Genug! Zum Schluss!

Sachs.

(To Walter.)

Sing, 'spite the Marker's angry mood!

Beckmesser.

(As Walter recommences, fetches out his board from the box and shows it, during the following, first to one and then to another, to convince the Masters, whom he at last gathers into a circle round him while he continues to exhibit his slate.)

What rubbish is this to shock us?
He surely means to mock us!
Every fault, both grave and slight,
I have marked on the board aright.
" Faulty verses," " Unsingable phrases,"
" Word-clippings," and " Vices " grave,
" Equivocal," " Rhymes in wrong places,"
" Reserved," " Displaced " is all the Stave.
A " Patch-work-Song " between the two verses,
" Clouded meaning " in every part,
" Uncertain words," then a " Change," that worse is,
There 's " Breath ill-managed," here 's " Sudden start,"
" Incomprehensible melody,"
A hotch-potch, made of all tones that be.
If at such toil you do not halt,
Masters, count after me each fault.
Already with the eight he was spent,
But so far as this sure none ever went!
Well over fifty, roughly told.
Say, would you this man a master hold?

The Masters.

(To one another.)

Ah yes, that 's true! 't is plain indeed,
That this young knight cannot succeed.
By Sachs he may be a genius thought,
But in our singing-school he is nought.
Who should in justice remain neglected,
If this novice a master were made?
If all the world's to be elected,
What good were the Masters' high grade?
Ha! look how the knight is enraged.
Hans Sachs on his side has engaged.
'T is really too bad! Quick make an end!
Up, Masters, speak and your hands extend!

Pogner.

(Aside.)

Ah yes, I see! 't is sad indeed:
My poor young knight will scarce succeed!
Should I retract my first decree,
I fear me sad results there 'd be.
I 'd fain see him no more neglected;
My kinship he would not degrade:
And when the victor is elected
Who knows if he will please my maid?
  Some trouble I presage,
  For Eva can I engage?

Sachs.

(Zu Walther.)

Singt, dem Herrn Merker zum Verdruss!

Beckmesser.

(Holt, während Walther beginnt, aus dem Gemerk die Tafel herbei, und hält sie während des Folgenden, von Einem zum Andern sich wendend, zur Prüfung den Meistern vor, die er schliesslich zu einem Kreis um sich zu vereinigen bemüht ist, welchem er immer die Tafel zur Einsicht vorhält.)

Was sollte man da noch hören?
Wär's nicht nur uns zu bethören?
Jeden der Fehler gross und klein,
Sehr genau auf der Tafel ein. —
" Falsch Gebänd," " unredbare Worte,"
" Kleb Sylben," hier " Laster " gar;
" Aequivoca," " Reim am falschen Orte,"
" Verkehrt," " verstellt " der ganze Bar;
Ein " Flickgesang " hier zwischen den Stollen;
" Blinde Meinung " allüberall;
" Unklare Wort'," " Differenz," hie " Schrollen,"
Da " falscher Athem," hier " Ueberfall."
Ganz unverständliche Melodei!
Aus allen Tönen ein Mischgebräu'!
Scheu'tet ihr nicht das Ungemach,
Meister, zählt mir die Striche nach!
Verloren hätt' er schon mit dem acht',
Doch so weit wie der hat's noch Keiner gebracht:
Wohl über fünfzig, schlecht gezählt!
Sagt, ob ihr euch den zum Meister wählt?

Die Meister.

(Durcheinander.)

Jo wohl, so ist's! Ich seh' es recht!
Mit dem Herrn Ritter steht es schlecht.
Mag Sachs von ihm halten, was er will,
Hier in der Singschul' schweig' er still!
Bleibt einem Jeden doch unbenommen,
Wen er zum Genossen begehrt?
Wär' uns der erste Best' willkommen,
Was blieben die Meister dann werth?
Hei! Wie sich der Ritter da quält!
Der Sachs hat ihn sich erwählt. —
's ist ärgerlich gar! Drum macht ein End'!
Auf Meister, stimmt und erhebt die Händ'!

Pogner.

(Für sich.)

Ja wohl, ich seh's, was mir nicht recht:
Mit meinem Junker steht es schlecht!
Weiche ich hier der Uebermacht,
Mir ahnet, dass mir's Sorge macht.
Wie gern säh' ich ihn angenommen,
Als Eidam wär' er mir gar werth;
Nenn' ich den Sieger nun willkommen,
Wer weiss, ob ihn mein Kind begehrt!
  Gesteh' ich's, dass mich das quält,
  Ob Eva den Meister wählt!

Walter.

(In wild and desperate enthusiasm, standing erect in the Singer's seat and looking down on commotion of the Masters.)

From gloomy thicket breaking
Behold the screech-owl swoop
With circling flight awaking
The ravens' croaking troop!
In sombre ranks they rise
And utter piercing cries;
With voices hoarse and hollow
The daws and magpies follow.
    Up then soars,
    By golden pinions stirr'd,
A wondrous lovely bird.
Each brightly glowing feather
Gleams in the glorious day;
It signs me hither — thither,
To float and flee away.
    The swelling heart,
    With pleasing smart,
Sore need with wings supplieth;
    It mounts in flight
    To giddy height,
    From the city's tomb,
    Through heaven's pure dome,
To hills of home it hieth,
Towards the verdant Vogelweid'
Where Master Walter lived and died;
    And there I'll rightly raise
    In song my lady's praise:
    Up shall soar,
When raven-Masters croak no more,
    My noble loving lay.
    Farewell, ye Masters, for aye!

(With a gesture of proud contempt he leaves the Singer's Seat and quits the building.)

Sachs.

(Following Walter's song.)
    Ha! what a flow
    Of genius' glow!
My Masters, pray now give o'er!
Listen, when Sachs doth implore!
Friend Marker, there! grant us some peace!
Let others listen! — Why won't you cease?
    No use! A vain endeavor!
I can scarcely my own voice hear!
    They'll heed the young fellow never:
He's bold indeed to persevere!
    His heart must be placed aright:
    A true born poet-knight! —
Hans Sachs may make both verse and shoe;
A knight is he and a poet, too.

The Prentices.

(Who have been rubbing their hands in glee and jump

Walther.

(In übermüthig verzweifelter Begeisterung, hoch auf dem Singstuhl aufgerichtet, und auf die unruhig durcheinander sich bewegenden Meister herabblickend.)

Aus finst'rer Dornenhecken
Die Eule rauscht' hervor,
Thät rings mit Kreischen wecken
Der Raben heis'ren Chor:
In nächt'gem Heer zu Hauf',
Wie krächzen all' da auf,
Mit ihren Stimmen, den hohlen,
Die Elstern, Kräh'n und Dohlen!
    Auf da steigt
    Mit gold'nem Flügelpaar,
Ein Vogel wunderbar:
Sein-strahlend hell Gefieder
Licht in den Lüften blinkt;
Schwebt selig hin und wieder,
Zu Flug und Flucht mir winkt
    Es schwillt das Herz
    Von süssem Schmerz,
Der Noth entwachsen Flügel;
    Es schwingt sich auf
    Zum kühnen Lauf,
    Zum Flug durch die Luft
    Aus der Städte Gruft,
Dahin zum heim'schen Hügel;
Dahin zur grünen Vogelweid',
Wo Meister Walther einst mich freit';
    Da sing' ich hell und hehr
    Der liebsten Frauen Ehr':
    Auf da steigt,
Ob Meister-Kräh'n ihm ungeneigt,
    Das stolze Minne-Lied. —
    Ade! ihr Meister, hienied'!

(Er verlässt mit einer stolz verächtlichen Gebärde des Stuhl und wendet sich zum Fortgehen.)

Sachs.

(Walther's Gesang folgend.)
    Ha, welch ein Muth!
    Begeistrungs-Gluth! —
Ihr Meister, schweigt doch und hört!
Hört, wenn Sachs euch beschwört!
Herr Merker da! gönnt doch nur Ruh'!
Lasst And're hören! gebt das nur zu! —
    Umsonst! All eitel Trachten!
Kaum vernimmt man sein eigen Wort!
    Des Junkers will Keiner achten: —
Das heiss' ich Muth, singt der noch fort!
    Das Herz auf dem rechten Fleck:
    Ein wahrer Dichter-Reck'!
Mach' ich, Hans Sachs, wohl Vers und Schuh',
Ist Ritter der und Poet dazu.

Die Lehrbuben.

(Welche längst sich die Hände rieben und von der Bank

ing up from their bench, towards the end take hands and dance in a ring round the Marker's box.)

God speed your Master-singing,
And may you the prize soon be winning:
The wreath of flowers in silk so bright,
I hope it may fall to your lot, sir knight!

Beckmesser.   Now, Masters, give it tongue!

(Most of them hold up their hands.)

All the Masters.   Rejected and outsung!

(General confusion, augmented by the Prentices, who shoulder the benches and Marker's box, causing hindrance and disorder to the Masters who are crowding to the door. Sachs remains alone in front, looking pensively at the empty seat; when the boys remove this too he turns away with humorous gesture of discouragement, and the curtain falls.)

aufsprangen, schliessen jetzt gegen das Ende wieder ihrer Reihen und tanzen um das Gemerk.)

Glück auf zum Meistersingen,
Mög't ihr euch das Kränzlein erschwingen:
Das Blumenkränzlein aus Seiden fein,
Wird das dem Herrn Ritter beschieden sein?

Beckmesser.
Nun, Meister, kündet's an!
(Die Mehrzahl hebt die Hände auf.)

Alle Meister.
Versungen und verthan!

(Alles geht in Aufregung auseinander, lustiger Tumult der Lehrbuben, welche sich des Gemerkes und der Meisterbänke bemächtigen, wodurch Gedränge und Durcheinander der nach dem Ausgange sich wendenden Meister ensteht. — Sachs, der allein im Vordergrunde verblieben, blickt noch gedankenvoll nach dem leeren Singstuhl; als die Lehrbuben auch diesen erfassen, und Sachs darob mit humoristisch-unmuthiger Gebärde sich abwendet, fällt der Vorhang.)

SECOND ACT.

The stage represents in front the section of a street running across, intersected in the middle by a narrow alley which winds crookedly towards the back, so that in C are two corner houses, of which one, a handsome one, R, is that of Pogner, the other, simpler, L, is Sachs's shop. — A flight of several steps leads up to Pogner's door: porch sunk in, with stone seats. At side R a lime-tree shades the place before the house; green shrubs at its foot, surrounding a stone seat. — The entrance to Sachs's house is also towards the street; a divided door leads into the cobbler's workshop; close by, an elder-tree spreads its boughs over it. Two windows, one of the workshop, the other of an inner chamber, look on to the alley. (All houses in both street and alley must be practicable.)

Genial summer evening; during the first scene night gradually closes.

David is putting up the shutters outside. Other Prentices are doing the same for other houses.

Prentices

(as they work).

Midsummer day! Midsummer day!
Flowers and ribbons in goodly display!

David

(aside).

" The wreath of flowers in silk so fine,
Would that to-morrow it might be mine."

Magdalena

(coming out of Pogner's house with a basket on her arm
and seeking to approach David unperceived).

Hist! David!

David

(turning toward the alley).

Whom are you calling?
Get along with your foolish squalling!

Prentices.

David, what cheer?
Why so severe?
Turn round your skull,
If you 're not dull!
" Midsummer day! Midsummer day!"
And he can't see Mistress Lena right in his way!

ZWEITER AUFZUG.

Die Bühne stellt im Vordergrunde eine Strasse im Längendurchschnitte dar, welche in der Mitte von einer schmalen Gasse, nach dem Hintergrunde zu krumm abbiegend, durchschnitten wird, so dass sich in Front zwei Eckhäuser darbieten, von denen das eine, reichere, rechts — das Haus Pogner's, das andere, einfachere — links — das des Hans Sachs ist. — Zu Pogner's Hause führt von der vorderen Strasse aus eine Treppe von mehreren Stufen; vertiefte Thüre, mit Steinsitzen in den Nischen. Zur Seite ist der Raum, ziemlich nah an Pogner's Hause, durch eine dickstämmige Linde abgegränzt; grünes Gesträuch umgibt sie am Fuss, vor welchem auch eine Steinbank angebracht ist. — Der Eingang zu Sachsens Hause ist ebenfalls nach der vorderen Strasse zu gelegen: eine getheilte Ladenthüre führet hier unmittelbar in die Schusterwerkstatt; dicht dabei steht ein Fliederbaum, dessen Zweige bis über den Laden hereinhängen. Nach der Gasse zu hat das Haus noch zwei Fenster, von welchen das eine zur Werkstatt, das andere zu einer dahinterliegenden Kammer gehört. [Alle Häuser, namentlich auch die der engeren Gasse, müssen praktikabel sein.]

Heiterer Sommerabend, im Verlaufe der ersten Auftritte allmählich einbrechende Nacht.

David ist darüber her, die Fensterläden nach der Gasse zu von aussen zu schliessen. Andere Lehrbuben thun das Gleiche bei andern Häusern.

Lehrbuben

(während der Arbeit).

Johannistag! Johannistag!
Blumen und Bänder so viel man mag!

David

(für sich).

" Das Blumenkränzlein von Seiden fein,
Möcht' es mir balde beschieden sein!"

Magdalene

(ist mit einem Korbe am Arm aus Pogner's Haus gekommen und sucht David unbemerkt sich zu nähern).

Bst! David!

David

(nach der Gasse zu sich umwendend).

Ruft ihr schon wieder!
Singt allein eure dummen Lieder!

Lehrbuben.

David, was soll's?
Wär'st nicht so stolz,
Schaut'st besser um,
Wär'st nicht so dumm!
" Johannistag! Johannistag!"
Wie der nur die Jungfer Lene nicht kennen mag!

Magdalena.

David, listen! Turn round, my dear!

David.

Ah, Mistress Lena! You are here?

Magdalena

(pointing to her basket).

Here's something nice; peep in and see 't!
'T is all for my dear lad to eat.
Tell me though first, What of Sir Walter?
You counseled him well? Has the crown been
won?

David.

Ah, Mistress Lena, how I falter!
He was outsung and declared outdone.

Magdalena.

Rejected! Outdone!

David.

What ails you, dear one?

Magdalena

(snatching the basket away from David's outstretched
hand).

Hands off the basket!
Dare you to ask it!
Good lack! Our chevalier outdone!

(she hastens back into the house, wringing her hands in
despair.)

(David looks after her dumfounded)

Prentices

(who have stolen near and overheard, now advance to
David as if congratulating him).

Hail to the Prentice and his bride!
How well his wooing speeds!
We all have heard and seen beside:
She upon whom he feeds
Within his heart's true casket,
Has gone and refused him the basket!

David

(flying out).

Be off with you boys!
Give over your noise!

Prentices

(dancing round David).

Midsummer day! Midsummer day!
All go a-courting as they may.

Magdalene.

David! hör' doch! kehr' dich zu mir!

David.

Ach, Jungfer Lene! Ihr seid hier?

Magdalene

(auf ihren Korb deutend).

Bring' dir was Gut's! schau nur hinein!
Das soll für mein lieb' Schätzel sein —
Erst aber schnell, wie ging's mit dem Ritter?
Du riethest ihm gut? Er gewann den Kranz?

David.

Ach, Jungfer Lene! Da steht's bitter;
Der hat verthan und versungen ganz!

Magdalene.

Versungen? Verthan?

David.

Was geht s euch nur an?

Magdalene

(den Korb, nach welchem David die Hand ausstreckt, auf
tig zurückziehend).

Hand von der Taschen!
Nichts da zu naschen! —
Hilf Gott! Unser Junker verthan!

(Sie geht mit Gebärden der Trostlosigkeit nach dem Hause
zurück).

David

(sieht ihr verblüfft nach).

Die Lehrbuben

(welche unbemerkt näher geschlichen waren, gelauscht
hatten und sich jetzt, wie glückwünschend, David präsen-
tiren).

Heil, Heil zur Eh' dem jungen Mann!
Wie glücklich hat er gefrei't!
Wir hörten's All', und sahen's an
Der er sein Herz geweiht,
Für die er lässt sein Leben,
Die hat ihm den Korb nicht gegeben.

David

(auffahrend).

Was steht ihr hier faul?
Gleich haltet eu'r Maul!

Die Lehrbuben.

(David umtanzend).

Johannistag! Johannistag!
Da frei't ein Jeder wie er mag.

The Masters woo,
And workmen too,
Old folks as well as the babbies!
And graybeards grim
Wed maidens slim,
Young fellows wed ancient tabbies.
Hooray! Hooray! Midsummer day!

(David is about to fly at the boys in his rage, when Sachs, who had come down the alley, steps between them. The Prentices separate.)

Sachs.

What now? Are you again in a fray?

David.

Not I! They sang a mocking stave.

Sachs.

Pay no heed; show how to behave!
Get in! To bed! Shut up and light!

David.

Have I to sing, sir?

Sachs.

                    Not to-night!
As punishment for to-day's offending,
Put all these shoes on the lasts for mending.

(Both go into the workshop and exeunt through an inner door. The Prentices have also dispersed.)

(Pogner and Eva, as if returning from a walk, come silently and thoughtfully down the alley, the daughter leaning on her father's arm.)

Pogner

(still in the alley, peeping through a chink in Sachs' shutter).

Let 's see if Sachs is in to-night;
I 'd speak with him. Suppose I call!

(David comes out of the inner room with a light and sits down to work at the bench by the window.)

Eva.

He seems at home : I see a light.

Pogner.

Shall I? Why should I after all?
                    (Turns away.)
If strange things I should venture,
Might I not earn his censure?
                    (After some reflection.)
Who said that I went too far? 'T was he,
    Yet, if our rules I exceeded,
    I have but done as he did!
But that might be mere vanity.
                    (To Eva.)
And you, my child, your thoughts are hid?

Der Meister freit!
Der Bursche freit!
Da gibt's Geschlamb' und Geschlumbfer!
Der Alte freit
Die junge Maid,
Der Bursche die alte Jungfer!—
Juchhei! Juchhei! Johannistag!

David ist im Begriff, wüthend drein zu schlagen, als Sachs, der aus der Gasse hervorgekommen, dazwischen tritt. Die Buben fahren auseinander.

Sachs.

Was gibt's? Treff' ich dich wieder am Schlag?

David.

Nicht ich! Schandlieder singen die.

Sachs.

Hör' nicht drauf! Lern's besser wie sie!
Zur Ruh'! in's Haus! Schliess' und mach Licht!

David.

Hab' ich noch Singstund'?

Sachs.

                    Nein, singst nicht!
Zur Straf' für dein heutig' frech' Erdreisten. —
Die neuen Schuh' steck' auf den Leisten!

(Sie sind Beide in die Werkstatt eingetreten und gehen durch innere Thüren ab. Die Lehrbuben haben sich ebenfalls zerstreut.)

Pogner und Eva; wie vom Spaziergange heimkehrend, die Tochter leicht am Arme des Vaters eingehenkt, sind beide schweigsam und in Gedanken die Gasse heraufgekommen.

Pogner

(noch auf der Gasse, durch eine Klinse im Fensterladen von Sachsens Werkstatt spähend).

Lass' sehn, ob Nachbar Sachs zu Haus?
Gern spräch' ich ihn. Trät' ich wohl ein?

(David kommt mit Licht aus der Kammer, setzt sich damit an den Werktisch am Fenster und macht sich über die Arbeit her.)

Eva.

Er scheint daheim : kommt Licht heraus.

Pogner.

Thu' ich's?—Zu was doch!—Besser, nein!
                    (Er wendet sich ab.)
Will Einer Selt'nes wagen,
Was liess' er da sich sagen?——
                    (Nach einigem Sinnen.)
War er's nicht, der meint', ich ging zu weit?
    Und blieb ich nicht im Geleise.
    War's nicht in seiner Weise?—
Doch war's vielleicht auch — Eitelkeit?'
                    (Zu Eva.)
Und du, mein Kind, du sagst mir nichts?

Eva.

Good children only speak when bid.

Pogner.

How sharp; how good! Come now, my wench,
And sit beside me on this bench.

(Sits on the stone seat under the linden-tree.)

Eva.

    Too chill to stay;
    'T was close all day.

Pogner.

    Oh, no! 't is mild and charming;
    The evening air is calming.

      (Eva sits, nervously.)

A token of a morrow fair
    And brilliant in its weather.
Oh, child, does not thy heart declare
The joys that morrow doth prepare,
When Nuremberg — yes, all the town,
    Both rich and poor together,
The guilds, the burghers of renown,
    Will meet in highest feather,
      To see thee rise
      And give the prize
    To him, the Master's head,
    To whom thou shalt be wed?

Eva.

Dear father, can but a Master win?

Pogner.

Be sure a Master is your fate.

(Magdalena appears at the door and signs to Eva.)

Eva

    (disturbed).

Aye — 't is my fate. — But now come in —
Yes, Lena, yes! — our suppers wait.

Pogner

    (rising vexedly).

But we have no guest?

Eva

    (as before).
    Not Sir Walter?

Pogner

    (surprised).
    Hey, what?

Eva.

Did you not meet?

Eva.

Ein folgsam Kind, gefragt nur spricht's.

Pogner.

Wie klug! Wie gut! — Komm', setz' dich hier
Ein Weil' noch auf die Bank zu mir.

(Er setzt sich auf die Steinbank unter der Linde.)

Eva.

    Wird's nicht zu kühl?
    's war heut' gar schwül.

Pogner.

    Nicht doch, 's ist mild und labend;
    Gar lieblich lind der Abend.

      (Eva setzt sich beklommen.)

Das deutet auf den schönsten Tag,
    Der morgen dir soll scheinen.
O Kind, sagt dir kein Herzensschlag,
Welch' Glück dich morgen treffen mag,
Wenn Nürnberg, die ganze Stadt
    Mit Bürgern und Gemeinen.
Mit Zünften, Volk und hohem Rath,
    Vor dir sich soll vereinen,
      Dass du den Preis,
      Das edle Reis,
    Ertheilest als Gemahl
    Dem Meister deiner Wahl.

Eva.

Lieb' Vater, muss es ein Meister sein?

Pogner.

Hör' wohl: ein Meister deiner Wahl.

(Magdalene erscheint an der Thür und winkt Eva.

Eva

    (zerstreut).

Ja, — meiner Wahl. — Doch, tritt nun ein —
Gleich, Lene, gleich! — zum Abendmahl.

Pogner

    (ärgerlich aufstehend).

's giebt doch keinen Gast?

Eva

    (wie oben).
    Wohl den Junker?

Pogner

    (verwundert).
    Wie so?

Eva.

Sahet ihn heute nicht?

Pogner

(half to himself).

I want him not.
Why, no !—What now?—Ah ! dare I guess?

Eva.

Dear father, come in and change your dress.

Pogner

(going into the house before her).

Hum !—What way does my fancy go?

(Exit.)

Magdalena

(secretly).

Why do you wait?

Eva.

(the same).

Be still ! speak low !

Magdalena.

Saw David !—says that he has n't won.

Eva.

Sir Walter?—O heavens ! what 's to be done?
Ah, Lena, I quake ; who will disclose all?

Magdalena.

Perhaps Hans Sachs?

Eva.

Ah, he 's fond of me !
'T is well, I will go

Magdalena.

Mind not to expose all !
If you stay longer your father will see.
When we 've supped : another thing I 'll unfold
thee ;
A secret which some one has just now told me.

Eva

Who was 't? Sir Walter?

Magdalena.

Not he, nay !
Beckmesser.

Eva.

Worth hearing I should say !

(They go into the house.)

(Sachs, in light indoor dress, has reëntered the workshop.
He turns to David, who is still at his workbench.)

Pogner

(halt für sich).

Ward sein nicht froh. —
Nicht doch !—Was denn?—Ei ! werd' ich dumm?

Eva.

Lieb' Väterchen, komm' ! Geh', kleid' dich um !

Pogner

(voran in das Haus gehend).

Hm !—Was geht mir im Kopf doch 'rum?

(Ab.)

Magdalene

(heimlich).

Hast was heraus?

Eva

(ebenso).

Blieb still und stumm.

Magdalene.

Sprach David : meint', er habe verthan.

Eva.

Der Ritter !—Hilf Gott, was fing' ich an !
Ach, Lene ! die Angst : wo 'was erfahren?

Magdalene.

Vielleicht vom Sachs !

Eva.

Ach, der hat mich lieb !
Gewiss, ich geh' hin,

Magdalene.

Lass drin nichts gewahren !
Der Vater merkt' es, wenn man jetzt blieb'. —
Nach dem Mahl ; dann hab' ich dir noch 'was zu
sagen
Was Jemand geheim mir aufgetragen.

Eva.

Wer denn? Der Junker?

Magdalene.

Nichts da ! Nein !
Beckmesser.

Eva.

Das mag 'was Rechtes sein!

(Sie gehen in das Haus.)

Sachs ist, in leichter Hauskleidung, in die Werkstatt
zurückgegangen. Er wendet sich zu David, der an seinem
Werktisch verblieben ist.

Sachs.

Come here ! — that 's right. — There by the door
Put my stool and workbench before ;
Then get to bed and early rise ;
Sleep off your folly, to-morrow be wise !

David
      (arranging bench and stool).

Are you still working?

Sachs.
                  What 's that to you?

David
          (aside).

What ailed Magdalena? — Would I knew !
And why works my Master by this light?

Sachs.

Why wait you?

David.
      Good-night, Master !

Sachs.
                  Good-night !

      (Exit David into the inner room.)

Sachs

(arranges his work, sits on his stool at the door and then,
laying down his tools again, leans back, resting his arm on
the closed lower half of the door).

      The elder's scent is waxing
      So mild, so full and strong?
      Its charm my limbs relaxing :
      Words unto my lips would throng. —
What boot such thoughts as I can span?
I 'm but a poor, plain-minded man !
      When work 's despised altogether,
      Thou, friend, settest me free ;
      But I 'd better stick to my leather
      And let all this poetry be ! —

      (He tries again to work. Leaves off and reflects.)

      And yet — it haunts me still. —
      I feel, but comprehend ill ; —
Cannot forget it, — and yet cannot grasp it. —
I measure it not e'en when I clasp it. —
      But how then would I gauge it?
      'T was measureless to my mind ;
      No rule could fit it or cage it,
      Yet there was no fault to find.
It seemed so old, yet new in its chime, —
Like songs of birds in sweet Maytime : —
      He who heard
      And, fancy-stirr'd,
      Sought to repeat the strain,
      But shame and scorn would gain —

Sachs.

Zeig' her ! — 's ist gut. — Dort an die Thür
Rück' mir Tisch und Schemel herfür ! —
Leg' dich zu Bett ! Wach' auf bei Zeit,
Verschlaf' die Dummheit, sei morgen gescheit !

David
      (richtet Tisch und Schemel).

Schafft ihr noch Arbeit?

Sachs.
               Kümmert dich das!

David
          (für sich).

Was war nur der Lene? — Gott weiss, was ! —
Warum wohl der Meister heute wacht !

Sachs.

Was steh'st noch?

David.
           Schlaft wohl, Meister !

Sachs.
                  Gut Nacht !

      (David geht in die Kammer ab.)

Sachs

(legt sich die Arbeit zurecht, setzt sich an der Thüre auf
den Schemel, lässt dann die Arbeit wieder liegen, und lehnt
mit dem Arm auf den geschlossenen Untertheil des Ladens
gestützt, sich zurück).

      Wie duftet doch der Flieder
      So mild, so stark und voll !
      Mir lös't es weich die Glieder,
      Will, das ich was sagen soll. —
Was gilt's, was ich dir sagen kann?
Bin gar ein arm einfältig Mann !
      Soll mir die Arbeit nicht schmecken,
      Gäb'st, Freund, lieber mich frei :
      Thät' besser das Leder zu strecken,
      Und liess' alle Poeterei ! —

      (Er versucht wieder zu arbeiten. Lässt ab und sinnt.)

      Und doch, 's will halt nicht geh'n. —
      Ich fühl's — und kann's nicht versteh'n —
Kann's nicht behalten, — doch auch nicht ver-
                    gessen ;
Und fass' ich es ganz, — kann ich's nicht messen. —
      Doch wie auch wollt' ich's fassen
      Was unermesslich mir schien?
      Kein' Regel wollte da passen,
      Und war doch kein Fehler drin. —
Es klang so alt, und war so neu, —
Wie Vogelsang im süssen Mai :
      Wer ihn hört,
      Und wahnbethört
      Sänge dem Vogel nach,
      Dem brächt' es Spott und Schmach.

Spring's command
And gentle hand
His soul with this did entrust:
He sang because he must!
His power rose as needed;
That virtue well I heeded.
The bird who sang to-day
Has got a throat that rightly waxes;
Masters may feel dismay,
But well content with him Hans Sachs is.

Eva comes out into the street, peeps shyly towards the workshop and advances unnoticed to the door by SACHS.

Eva.

Good-evening, Master! Still at labor?

Sachs
(starting up in agreeable surprise).

Ah, child! Sweet Eva! still about?
And yet I guess the cause, fair neighbor:
The new-made shoes?

Eva.
How far you 're out!
The shoes I have not even essay'd;
They are so fine, so richly made,
I dare not such gems to my feet confide.

Sachs.

You 'll wear them, though, to-morrow as bride?

Eva
(who has now seated herself on the stone seat by Sachs).

Who is to be the bridegroom, then?

Sachs.
Can I tell?

Eva.
How know you I 'm to be bride?

Sachs.
Eh, well!
Ev'ry one knows.

Eva.
Aye, ev'ry one knows.
That 's proof positive, I suppose
I thought you knew more.

Sachs.
What should I know?

Eva.
See there! Must I my meaning show?
How dull I must be!

Sachs.
I say not so.

Lenzes Gebot,
Die süsse Noth,
Die legten's ihm in die Brust:
Nun sang er, wie er musst'!
Und wie er musst', so konnt' er's;
Das merkt' ich ganz besonders:
Dem Vogel, der heut' sang,
Dem war der Schnabel hold gewachsen;
Macht' er den Meistern bang,
Gar wohl gefiel er doch Hans Sachsen.

Eva ist auf die Strasse getreten, hat schüchtern spähend sich der Werkstatt genähert, und steht jetzt unvermerkt an der Thüre bei Sachs.

Eva.

Gut'n Abend, Meister! Noch so fleissig?

Sachs
(ist angenehm überrascht aufgefahren).

Ei, Kind! Lieb' Evchen? Noch so spät?
Und doch, warum so spät noch, weiss ich:
Die neuen Schuh'?

Eva.
Wie fehl er räth!
Die Schuh' hab' ich noch gar nicht probirt;
Die sind so schön, so reich geziert,
Dass ich sie noch nicht an die Füss' mir getraut.

Sachs.

Doch sollst sie morgen tragen als Braut?

Eva
(hat sich dicht bei Sachs auf den Steinsitz gesetzt).

Wer wäre denn Bräutigam?

Sachs.
Weiss ich das?

Eva.
Wie wisst denn ihr, ob ich Braut?

Sachs.
Ei was!
Das weiss die Stadt.

Eva.
Ja, weiss es die Stadt,
Freund Sachs gute Gewähr dann hat.
Ich dacht', er wüsst' mehr.

Sachs.
Was sollt' ich wissen?

Eva.
Ei seht doch! Werd' ich's ihm sagen müssen?
Ich bin wohl recht dumm?

Sachs.
Das sagt' ich nicht.

Eva.

Then you must be bright?

Sachs.

That I don't know.

Eva.

You know naught! You say naught!
                    Ah, friend Sachs!
I see now clearly, pitch is not wax.
I really believ'd you were sharper.

Sachs.

                              My dear!
Both pitch and wax are well known here.
With wax I rubbed the silken stitching
With which I sewed your pretty shoes;
The thread for these coarser ones I 'm pitching;
'T is good enough for a man to use.

Eva.

Whom do you mean! Some grandee:

Sachs.

                              Aye, marry!
A Master proud who boldly woos,
Expecting to-morrow all to carry;
For Master Beckmesser I make these shoes.

Eva.

Then pitch in plenty let there be,
To stick him fast and leave me free.

Sachs.

He hopes by singing to attain thee.

Eva.

Why should he hope?

Sachs.

                    Why should he not?
Few bachelors are on the spot.

Eva.

Might not a widower hope to gain me?

Sachs.

My child, I am too old for you.

Eva.

Ah, stuff! too old! Art is the thing;
Who masters that is free to woo.

Sachs.

Dear Eva, are you flattering?

Eva.

Dann wär't ihr whol klug?

Sachs.

                    Das weiss ich nicht

Eva.

Ihr wisst nichts? Ihr sagt nichts? — Ei, Freund
                              Sachs!
Jetzt merk' ich wahrlich, Pech ist kein Wachs.
Ich hätt' euch für feiner gehalten.

Sachs.

                              Kind!
Beid', Wachs und Pech vertraut mir sind.
Mit Wachs strich ich die Seidenfäden,
Damit ich die zieren Schuh' dir gefasst:
Heut' fass ich die Schuh' mit dicht'ren Drähten,
Da gilt's mit Pech für den derben Gast.

Eva.

Wer ist denn der? Wohl 'was Rechts?

Sachs.

                    Das mein' ich!
Ein Meister stolz auf Freiers Fuss,
Denkt morgen zu siegen ganz alleinig:
Herrn Beckmesser's Schuh' ich richten muss.

Eva.

So nehmt nur tüchtig Pech dazu:
Da kleb' er drin, und lass' mir Ruh'!

Sachs.

Er hofft dich sicher zu ersingen.

Eva.

Wie so denn der?

Sachs.

                              Ein Junggesell:
's gibt deren wenig dort zur Stell'.

Eva.

Könnt's einem Wittwer nicht gelingen?

Sachs.

Mein Kind der wär' zu alt für dich.

Eva.

Ei was, zu alt! Hier gilt's die Kunst:
Wer sie versteht, der werb' um mich!

Sachs.

Lieb' Evchen! Machst mir blauen Dunst?

Eva.

Not I ; 't is you are an impostor !
Admit now, your affections veer ;
Heav'n knows whom now your heart may foster !
I 'd thought it my own this many a year.

Sachs.

Because in my arms I oft carried you ?

Eva.

I see. You had no child of your own.

Sachs.

I once had wife and children too.

Eva.

But they are dead and I am grown.

Sachs.

Grown tall and fair.

Eva.

'T was my idea
That I might fill their places here.

Sachs.

Then I should have child and also wife :
That were indeed a joy in life !
Aye, that was an idea I vow !

Eva.

I think you 're trying to mock me now.
In short, 't would give you little sorrow
If under your nose from all to-morrow,
This Beckmesser sang me away !

Sachs.

If he succeeded what could I say !
'T would rest on what your father said.

Eva.

Where does a Master keep his head ?
Were I with you could it be found ?

Sachs.

Ah, yes ! you 're right ! all my brain turns round.
I 've been annoyed and vexed to-day,
And in my mind some traces stay.

Eva.

Aye, in the Song-school ? You met, I see.

Sachs.

Yes, child ; an election has worried me.

Eva.

Nicht ich ! Ihr seid's ; ihr macht mir Flausen !
Gesteht nur, dass ihr wandelbar ;
Gott weiss, wer jetzt euch im Herzen mag hausen !
Glaubt' ich mich doch drin so manches Jahr.

Sachs.

Wohl, da ich dich gern in den Armen trug ?

Eva.

Ich seh', 's war nur, weil ihr kinderlos.

Sachs.

Hatt' einst Weib und Kinder genug.

Eva.

Doch starb eure Frau, so wuchs ich gross.

Sachs.

Gar gross und schön !

Eva.

Drum dacht' ich aus.
Ihr nähm't mich für Weib und Kind in's Haus.

Sachs.

Da hätt' ich ein Kind und auch ein Weib :
's wär' gar ein lieber Zeitvertreib !
Ja, ja ! das hast du dir schön erdacht.

Eva.

Ich glaub', der Meister mich gar verlacht ?
Am End' gar liess' er sich auch gefallen,
Dass unter der Nas' ihm weg von Allen
Der Beckmesser morgen mich ersäng' ?

Sachs.

Wie sollt, ich's wehren, wenn's ihm geläng' ? —
Dem wüsst' allein dein Vater Rath.

Eva.

Wo so ein Meister den Kopf nur hat !
Käm' ich zu euch wohl, fänd' ich's zu Haus ?

Sachs.

Ach, ja ! Hast Recht ! 's ist im Kopf mir kraus :
Hab' heut' manch' Sorg' und Wirr erlebt :
Da mag's dann sein, dass 'was drin klebt.

Eva.

Wohl in der Singschul'? 's war' heut' Gebot

Sachs.

Ja, Kind : eine Freiung machte mir Noth.

Eva.

O Sachs! but you should at once have said so,
Then my tongue would not have plagued your
head so.
Now say, who was it entrance besought?

Sachs.

A knight, my child, and quite untaught.

Eva.

A knight? Dear me! And did he succeed?

Sachs.

Why, no, my child, we disagreed.

Eva.

Dear me! how strange! relate it, pray;
If you are vexed, can I be gay?
Then he was defeated and baffled quite?

Sachs.

Truly hopeless the case of the noble knight.

Magdalena

    (comes to the house-door and calls softly).

Hist! Eva! Hist!

Eva.

          Truly hopeless! And why?
Were there no means to help him by?
Sang he so ill, so faultily
He never a Master can hope to be?

Sachs.

My child, it is a hopeless disaster;
No leader he 'll be in any land;
For when one is born to be a Master,
'Mong other Masters he cannot stand.

Magdalena

    (approaching).

Your father awaits.

Eva.

         But tell me the end,
If none of the Masters he won for a friend?

Sachs

That is a good joke! friend could we call
One before whom we all felt so small?
My young lord Haughty, let him toddle,
In the world to cool his noddle.
What we have learnt with toil and care,
Let us digest in peace unhurried!
Here we must by none be worried:
So let his fortune shine elsewhere!

Eva.

Ja, Sachs! Das hättet ihr gleich soll'n sagen;
Plagt' euch dann nicht mit unnützen Fragen. —
Nun sagt, wer war's, der Freiung begehrt?

Sachs.

Ein Junker, Kind, gar unbelehrt.

Eva.

Ein Junker! Mein, sagt! — und ward er gefreit?

Sachs.

Nichts da, mein Kind! 's gab zu viel Streit.

Eva.

So Sagt! Erzählt wie ging es zu?
Macht's euch Sorg', wie liess' mir es Ruh'?
So bestand er übel und hat verthan?

Sachs.

Ohne Gnad' versang der Herr Rittersmann.

Magdalene

    (kommt zum Haus heraus und ruft leise).

Bst! Evchen! Bst!

Eva.

          Ohne Gnade? Wie
Kein Mittel gäb's, das ihm gadieh'?
Sang er so schlecht, so fehlervoll,
Dass nichts mehr zum Meister ihm helfen soll?

Sachs.

Mein Kind, für den ist Alles verloren,
Und Meister wird der in keinem Land;
Denn wer als Meister ward geboren,
Der hat unter Meistern den schlimmsten Stand.

Magdalene

    (näher).

Der Vater verlangt.

Eva.

         So sagt mir noch an,
Ob keinen der Meister zum Freund er gewann?

Sachs.

Das wär nicht übel! Freund ihm noch sein!
Ihm, vor dem All' sich fühlen so klein!
Den Junker Hochmuth, lasst ihn laufen,
Mag er durch die Welt sich raufen:
Was wir erlent mit Noth und Müh',
Dafei lasst uns in Ruh' verschnaufen!
Hier renn' er nichts uns über'n Haufen ·
Sein Glück ihm anderswo erblüh'!

Eva.

(rising hastily).

Yes, elsewhere it will shine, I know,
In spite of what your envious pack says;
Some place where hearts still warmly glow,
With no deceitful Master Sachses!—
Yes, Lena! Yes! I'm coming, dear!—
Nice consolation I get here!
I smell the pitch, Heav'n keep us whole!
Burn it, rather, and warm up your soul.

(She crosses over hastily with Magdalena and remains in
agitation at her own door.)

Sachs

(with a meaning nod of his head).

I thought as much! Now then they'll prate!

(During the following he closes the upper half of his door
also, so nearly as only to leave a little crack of light, he
himself being quite invisible.)

Magdalena.

Good lack! why have you stayed so late?
Your father called.

Eva.

                    Go you instead,
And say that I am gone to bed.

Magdalena.

No, no! Hark now! I have news too!
Beckmesser found me; such a to-do!
To-night, if but at the window stay'd you,
He said he would come and serenade you.
The song he intends for your winning he'll sing,
To try if your approval 't will bring.

Eva.

He need not trouble!—where can he be?

Magdalena.

Has David been here?

Eva.

                    What's that to me?

Magdalena

(half to herself).

I was too harsh; he's vexed, I fear.

Eva.

No one in sight?

Magdalena.

Some one draws near.

Eva.

Is 't he?

Eva

(erhebt sich heftig).

Ja, anderswo soll's ihm erblüh'n,
Als bei euch garst'gen, neid'schen Mannsen!
Wo warm die Herzen noch erglüh'n,
Trotz allen tück'schen Meister Hansen!
Ja, Lene! Gleich! ich komme schon!
Was trüg' ich hier für Trost davon?
Da riecht's nach Pech, dass Gott erbarm'!
Brennt' er's lieber, da würd er doch warm!

Sie geht heftig mit Magdalene hinüber und verweilt sehr
aufgeregt dort unter der Thüre.

Sachs.

(nickt bedeutungsvoll mit dem Kopfe).

Das dacht' ich wohl. Nun heisst's: schaff' Rath!

Er ist während des Folgenden damit beschäftigt, auch die
obere Ladenthüre so weit zu schliessen, dass sie nur ein
wenig Licht noch durchlässt; er selbst verschwindet so fast
ganz.

Magdalene.

Hilf Gott! was bliebst du nur so spat?
Der Vater rief.

Eva.

                    Geh' zu ihm ein:
Ich sei zu Bett im Kämmerlein.

Magdalene.

Nicht doch! Hör' nur! Komm' ich dazu?
Beckmesser fand mich: er lässt nicht Ruh',
Zur nacht sollst du dich an's Fenster neigen,
Er will dir 'was Schönes singen und geigen,
Mit dem er dich hofft zu gewinnen, das Lied,
Ob dir das zu Gefallen gerieth.

Eva.

Das fehlte auch noch!—Käme nur Er!

Magdalene.

Hast' David geseh'n?

Eva

                    Was soll mir der?

Magdalene

(halb für sich).

Ich war zu streng; er wird sich grämen.

Eva.

Siehst du noch nichts?

Magdalene.

                    's ist als ob Leut' dort kämen.

Eva.

Wär' er's?

Magdalena.

            Come ; 't is time to depart.

Eva.

Not till I 've seen the man of my heart.

Magdalena.

I made a mistake, it is not he.
Come in, for fear your father should see.

Eva.

What shall I do?

Magdalena.

              We 'll hold consultation
As to this Beckmesser's invitation.

Eva.

Stand you at the window for me.

Magdalena.

                  What, I?
'T would rouse poor David's jealousy.
He sleeps on the street side.   He he ! what fun !

Eva.

I hear a footstep !

Magdalena.

              Come now, let us run !

Eva.

It nears us !

Magdalena.

           You 're wrong, I 'll bet my head.
Do come ! You must, till your father 's in bed.

Pogner

          (calling within).

Hey ! Lena ! Eva !

Magdalena.

            No more delay !
D' ye hear? Come — your knight 's far away.

Walter has come up the alley and now turns the corner
by Pogner's house. Eva, who is being dragged indoors by
Magdalena, tears herself free with a slight cry and rushes
towards Walter.

Eva.

It is he !

Magdalena.

         (going in).

           Now all 's up.   Be quick, I say !

         (Exit).

Magdalene.

           Mach' und komm' jetzt hinan !

Eva.

Nicht eh'r, bis ich sah den theuersten Mann !

Magdalene.

Ich täuschte mich dort : er war es nicht.
Jetzt komm, sonst merkt der Vater die G'schicht' !

Eva.

Ach ! meine Angst !

Magdalene.

            Auch lass uns berathen,
Wie wir des Beckmesser's uns entladen.

Eva.

Zum Fenster gehst du für mich.

Magdalene.

                Wie. ich?
Das machte wohl David eiferlich !
Er schläft nach der Gassen ! Hihi ! 's wär' fein ! —

Eva.

Dort hör' ich Schritte.

Magdalene.

           Jetzt komm', es muss sein !

Eva.

Jetzt näher !

Magdalene.

          Du irrst ! 's ist nichts, ich wett'.
Ei, komm' !   Du musst, bis der Vater zu Bett.

Pogner

         (von innen rufend).

He ! Lene ! Eva !

Magdalene

          's ist höchste Zeit !
Hörst du's? — Komm' ! — der Ritter ist Weit. —

Walther ist die Gasse heraufgekommen; jetzt biegt er um
Pogner's Haus herum; Eva, die bereits von Magdalene am
Arm hineingezogen worden war, reisst sich mit einem leisen
Schrei los und stürzt Walther entgegen.

Eva.

Da ist er !

Magdalene

         (hineingehend).

Nun haben wir's !   Jetzt heisst's gescheit !

         (Ab.)

Eva
(transported).

'T is my true love !
Yes, my own love !
Naught conceal I,
All is known, love :
All reveal I.
For I know it :
It is you, love,
Hero-Poet
And my only friend !

Walter
(sorrowfully).

Ah, thou 'rt wrong ! I 'm but thy friend ;
Not as Poet
Masters prize me,
For my station
They despise me :
Inspiration
They can brook not,
And — I know it —
I may look not
To my lady's hand !

Eva.

Thou art wrong ! Thy lady's hand
Awards the prize alone.
Thy courage doth my heart command ;
Be then the wreath thine own.

Walter.

Ah, no, thou 'rt wrong ! My lady's hand,
Though no one else should gain it.
Upon the terms thy father plann'd
I never may attain it.
" A Master-Singer he must be :
None may'st thou wed uncrowned by thee."
Thus to the Guild he firmly spake ;
What he hath pledged he may not break.
That spurred my heart's desire,
Though strange to me were place and folk :
I sang, all love and fire,
And strove to make a Master-stroke.

The loud sound of a night-watchman's cowhorn is heard.
Walter clasps his hand to his sword and stares wildly before
him.

Ha !

Eva
(taking him soothingly by the hand)

Belovĕd, govern thy wrath !
'T is but the watchman goes forth.—
Hide 'neath the lime-tree !
Lose no more time ! See,
The watchman passes this way.

Magdalena
(at the door, softly).

Eva ! 't is late : come in, I say !

Eva
(ausser sich).

Ja, ihr seid es !
Nein, du bist es
Alles sag' ich,
Denn ihr wisst es ;
Alles klag' ich,
Denn ich weiss es ;
Ihr seid Beides,
Held des Preises,
Und mein einz'ger Freund !

Walther
(leidenschaftlich).

Ach, du irrst ! Bin nur dein Freund,
Doch des Preises
Noch nicht würdig,
Nicht den Meistern
Ebenbürtig :
Mein Begeistern
Fand Verachten,
Und ich weiss es,
Darf nicht trachten
Nach der Freundin Hand !

Eva.

Wie du irrst ! Der Freundin Hand,
Ertheilt nur sie den Preis.
Wie deinen Muth ihr Herz erfand,
Reicht sie nur dir das Reis.

Walther.

Ach nein, du irrst ! Der Freundin Hand,
Wär Keinem sie erkoren,
Wie sie des Vaters Wille band,
Mir wär' sie doch verloren.
„ Ein Meistersinger muss er sein :
Nur wen ihr krönt, den darf sei frei'n !"
So sprach er festlich zu den Herrn,
Kann nicht zurück, möcht er's auch gern !
Das eben gab mir Muth ;
Wie ungewohnt mir alles schien,
Ich sang mit Lieb' und Gluth,
Dass ich den Meisterschlag verdien'.

Man hört den starken Ruf eines Nachtwächter hornes.
Walther legt mit emphatischer Gebärde die Hand an sein
Schwert, und starrt wild vor sich hin.

Ha ! . . .

Eva
(fasst ihn besänftigend an der Hand).

Geliebter, spare den Zorn !
's war nur des Nachtwächters Horn. —
Unter der Linde
Birg' dich geschwinde.
Hier kommt der Wächter vorbei.

Magdalene
(an der Thüre, leise).

Evchen ! 's ist Zeit, mach' dich frei !

Walter.

You fly?

Eva.

   Must I not flee?

Walter.

You fear—?

Eva.

   The powers that be!

(She disappears with Magdalena into the house.)

The Watchman

(has meanwhile appeared in the alley. He comes forward singing, turns the corner of Pogner's house and exit L).

" Hark to what I say, good people ;
Striketh ten from every steeple.
Put out your fire and eke your light,
That none may come to harm this night.
   Praise the Lord of Heav'n ! "

(He has by this time gone off, but his horn is still heard).

Sachs

(who has listened to the foregoing from behind his shop-door, now opens it a little wider, having shaded his lamp).

Pretty doings now are in hand !
Here 's an elopement being plann'd.
I 'm awake !   This must not be.

Walter

   (behind the lime-tree).

Has she then left me ?   Woe is me !—
Yet no ! who comes here ?— Ah, not she !
'T is Magdalena.— Yet surely !— *Thou!*

Eva

(returns in Magdalena's dress and goes to Walter).

Thy foolish child, she 's all thine now !

   (She sinks on his breast.)

Walter.

O heaven ! here before my eyes
I see indeed the Master-prize !

Eva.

   Now no more delay !
   Let 's hasten away !
  Oh, would that we were gone !

Walter.

   Here, through this alley : on !
   Servants at the gate
   With my horses wait.

Walther.

Du fliehst?

Eva.

   Muss ich denn nicht?

Walther.

Entweichst?

Eva.

   Dem Meistergericht.

(Sie verschwindet mit Magdalene im Hause.)

Der Nachtwächter.

(ist währenddem in der Gasse erschienen, kommt singend nach vorn, biegt um die Ecke von Pogner's Haus, und geht nach links zu weiter ab).

„ Hört ihr Leut' und lasst euch sagen,
Die Glock' hat Zehn geschlagen :
Bewahrt das Feuer und auch das Licht,
Damit Niemand kein Schad' geschicht !
   Lobet Gott den Herrn ! "

(Als er hiermit abgegangen, hört man ihn abermals blasen.

Sachs

(welcher hinter der Ladenthüre dem Gespräche gelauscht, öffnet jetzt, bei eingezogenem Lampenlicht, ein wenig mehr).

Ueble Dinge, die ich da merk' :
Eine Entführung gar im Werk !
Aufgepasst : das darf nicht sein !

Walther

   (hinter der Linde).

Käm' sie nicht wieder ?   O der Pein !—
Doch' ja ! sie kommt dort !   Weh' mir, nein !
Die Alte ist's !— doch aber — ja !

Eva

(ist in Magdalene's Kleidung wieder zurückgekehrt und geht auf Walther zu).

Das thör'ge Kind : da hast du's ! da !

   (Sie sinkt ihm an die Brust.

Walther.

O Himmel ! . Ja ! nun wohl ich weiss,
Dass ich gewann den Meisterpreis.

Eva.

   Doch nun kein Besinnen !
   Von hinnen !   Von hinnen !
  O wären wir weit schon fort !

Walther.

   Hier durch die Gasse : dort
   Finden wir vor dem Thor
   Knecht und Rosse vor.

As they turn to dive into the alley Sachs places his lamp behind a water-globe and sends a bright stream of light through the now wide-open door across the street, so that Eva and Walter suddenly find themselves illuminated.

Eva

(hastily pulling Walter back).

Ah me! the cobbler! What would he say!
Hide thee!—keep well out of his way!

Walter.

What other road leads to the gate?

Eva

(pointing R).

Round by the street here, but 't is not straight;
I know it not well; besides, we should meet
With the watchman.

Walter.

Well, then, through the alley!

Eva.

The cobbler must first leave his windowseat.

Walter.

I 'll force him then. Here 's for a sally!

Eva.

Shew not yourself: he knows you!

Walter.

Who is he?

Eva.

'T is Sachs!

Walter.

Hans Sachs? my friend?

Eva.

Not quite!

With slanders against you he is busy.

Walter.

What Sachs! He too?—I 'll put out his light!

Beckmesser comes up the alley slinking at some distance in the rear of the watchman. He peers up to Pogner's windows and, leaning against Sach's house, seeks out a stone seat on which he places himself, still looking at the upper windows, and now he commences to tune a lute he has brought with him.

Eva

(restraining Walter).

Forbear!—Now hark!

Walter.

A lute I hear.

Als sich Beide wenden, um die Gasse einzubiegen, lässt Sachs, nachdem er die Lampe hinter eine Glaskugel gestellt, einen hellen Lichtschein durch die ganz wieder geöffnete Ladenthüre, quer über die Strasse fallen, so dass Eva und Walther sich plötzlich hell erleuchtet sehen.

Eva

(Walther heftig zurückziehend).

O weh', der Schuster! Wenn der uns säh'!
Birg' dich? komm' ihm nicht in die Näh'!

Walther.

Welch' andrer Weg führt uns hinaus?

Eva

(nach rechts deutend).

Dort durch die Strasse: doch der ist kraus,
Ich kenn' ihn nicht gut; auch stiessen wir dort
Auf den Wächter.

Walther.

Nun denn: durch die Gasse!

Eva.

Der Schuster muss erst vom Fenster fort.

Walther.

Ich zwing' ihn dass er's verlasse.

Eva.

Zeig dich ihm nicht: er kennt dich!

Walther.

Der Schuster?

Eva.

's ist Sachs.

Walther.

Hans Sachs, mein Freund?

Eva.

Glaub's nicht!

Von dir zu sagen Uebles nur wusst' er.

Walther.

Wie, Sachs? Auch er?—Ich lösch' ihm das Licht!

Beckmesser ist, dem Nachtwächter in einiger Entfernung nachschleichend die Gasse herauf gekommen, hat nach den Fenstern von Pogner's Hause gespäht, und, an Sachsen's Hause angelehnt, zwischen den beiden Fenstern einen Steinsitz sich ausgesucht, auf welchem er sich, immer nur nach dem gegenüberliegenden Fenster aufmerksam lugend, niedergelassen hat; jetzt stimmt er eine mitgebrachte Laute.

Eva

(Walther zurückhaltend).

Thu's nicht!—Doch horch!

Walther.

Einer Laute Klang?

Eva.

What a mishap!

Walter.

Why need you fear?
The cobbler's light has ceased to glare:
Let 's make the attempt!

Eva.

Ah! see you not there?
Some other comes to spoil our plans.

Walter.

I hear and see: some player man.
What wants he here so late at night?

Eva.

'T is Beckmesser!

Sachs

(on hearing the first sounds of the lute has, as if struck with
a new idea, withdrawn his light, gently opened the lower
half of his shopdoor and placed his workbench on the
threshold. He now hears Eva's exclamation).

Aha! I 'm right!

Walter.

The Marker here? and placed in my pow'r?
Here goes! The fool shall rue this hour!

Eva.

O heav'n! Forbear! Would you wake my father?
He 'll sing his song and quit us then.
Let 's hide behind the foliage rather.
Oh, dear! what trouble you give, you men!

(She draws Walter behind the bushes which surround the
bench under the lime-tree.)

Beckmesser impatiently tinkles on his lute waiting for the
window to open. As he is about to commence his song
Sachs turns his light full on the street again and begins to
hammer loudly on his last, singing lustily the while.

Sachs.

Tooral looral!
Tiddy fol de rol!
Oho! Tralala! Oho!
When Mother Eve from Paradise
Was by the Almighty driven,
Her naked feet, so small and nice,
By stones were sorely riven.
This troubled much the Lord,
Her tootsies he ador'd
An angel he did straightway choose:
" Go make that pretty sinner shoes!
And as poor Adam limps around;
And breaks his toes on stony ground,
That well and wide
His legs may stride,
Measure him for boots beside!"

Eva.

Ach, meine Noth!

Walther.

Wie, wird dir bang?
Der Schuster, sieh, zog ein das Licht: —
So sei's gewagt!

Eva.

Weh'! Hörst du denn nicht?
Ein Andrer kam, und nahm dort Stand.

Walther.

Ich hör's und seh's: — ein Musikant.
Was will der hier so spät des Nachts?

Eva.

's ist Beckmesser schon!

Sachs

(als er den ersten Ton der Laute vernommen, hat, von einem
plötzlichen Einfal erfasst, das Licht wieder etwas eingezogen,
leise auch den unteren Theil des Ladens geöffnet, und
seinen Werktisch ganz unter die Thüre gestellt. Jetzt hat er
Eva's Ausruf vernommen).

Aha! ich dacht's!

Walther.

Der Merker? Er? in meiner Gewalt?
D'rauf zu, den Lung'rer mach' ich kalt?

Eva.

Um Gott! So hör'! Willst den Vater wecken?
Er singt ein Lied, dann zieht er ab.
Lass dort uns im Gebüsch verstecken. —
Was mit den Männern ich Müh' doch hab'!

(Sie zieht Walther hinter das Gebüsch auf die Bank unter der
Linde.)

Beckmesser

(klimpert voll Ungeduld heftig auf der Laute, ob sich das
Fenster nicht öffnen wolle. Als er endlich anfangen will zu
singen beginnt Sachs, der soeben das Licht wieder hell auf
die Strasse fallen liess, laut mit dem Hammer auf den
Leisten zu schlagen, und singt sehr kräftig dazu).

Sachs.

Jerum! Jerum!
Halla halla he!
O ho! Trallalei! o he!
Als Eva aus dem Paradies
Von Gott dem Herrn verstossen,
Gar schuf ihr Schmerz der harte Kiess
An ihrem Fuss, dem blossen.
Das jammerte den Herrn,
Ihr Füsschen hat er gern,
Und seinem Engel rief er zu:
„ Da mach' der armen Sünd'rin Schuh'!
Und da der Adam, wie ich seh',
An Steinen dort sich stösst die Zeh,
Dass recht fortan
Er wandeln kann,
So miss' dem auch Stiefel an!"

Beckmesser

(as Sachs begins to sing).

What is it now?
Atrocious row!
The vulgar cobbler 's drunk, I trow!

(Advancing.)

What, Master! Up, so long after dark?

Sachs.

You also out, Master Town-clerk?
The shoes perhaps on your mind are weighing?
You see me at work: I 'm not delaying.

Beckmesser.

Deuce take boot and shoe!
Be quiet do!

Walter

(to Eva).

What is that song? He speaks of thee.

Eva.

I know it well; he means not me.
But hidden malice here I trace.

Walter.

What vile delay! Time flies apace!

Sachs

(working).

Tooral looral!
Tiddy fol de rol!
Oho! Tralala! Oho!
O Eve! Hear how my poor heart aches,
By grief and trouble sodden;
The works of Art a cobbler makes
All under foot are trodden.
Did not an angel bring
For such work comforting,
And call me oft to Heaven's gate,
I 'd quickly leave this trade I hate!
But when he takes me up on high,
The world beneath my feet doth lie:
Then rest doth woo
Hans Sachs, the shoe-
Maker and the Poet too.

Beckmesser

(watching the window which now opens softly).

The window 's unclosed! — O heavens! 't is she!

Eva

(to Walter).

Why does that song dispirit me?
Oh, hence, let us hasten!

Beckmesser

(alsbald nach Beginn des Verses).

Was soll das sein? —
Verdammtes Schrein!
Was fällt dem groben Schuster ein?

(Vortretend.)

Wie, Meister? Auf? So spät zur Nacht?

Sachs.

Herr Stadtschreiber! Was, ihr wacht? —
Die Schuh' machen euch grosse Sorgen?
Ihr seht, ich bin dran: ihr habt sie morgen.

Beckmesser.

Hol' der Teufel die Schuh'!
Ich will hier Ruh'!

Walther

(zu Eva).

Wie heisst das Leid? Wie nennt er dich?

Eva.

Ich hört' es schon: 's geht nicht auf mich,
Doch eine Bosheit steckt darin.

Walther.

Welch' Zögerniss! Die Zeit geht hin!

Sachs

(fortarbeitend).

Jerum! Jerum!
Halla halla he!
O ho! Trallalei! O he!
O Eva! Hör' mein Klageruf,
Mein Noth und schwer Verdrüssen!
Die Kunstwerk', die ein Schuster schuf,
Sie tritt die Welt mit Füssen!
Gäb nicht ein Engel Trost,
Der gleiches Werk erlos't,
Und rief mich oft in's Paradies,
Wie dann ich Schuh' und Stiefel liess'!
Doch wenn der mich im Himmel hält,
Dann liegt zu Füssen mir die Welt,
Und bin in Ruh'
Hans Sachs ein Schuh-
macher und Poet dazu.

Beckmesser

(das Fenster gewahrend, welches jetzt sehr leise geöffnet
wird).

Das Fenster geht auf: — Herr Gott, 's ist sie!

Eva

(zu Walther).

Mich schmerzt das Lied, ich weiss nicht wie!
O fort, lass uns fliehen!

Walter

(half-drawing his sword).

But one way remains !

Eva.

Oh, no !   Forbear !

Walter.

He 's scarce worth the pains !

Eva.

Yes, patience is best.   O dearest love,
That I should such a trouble prove !

Walter.

Who 's at the window ?

Eva.

'T is Magdalena.

Walter.

That 's real retribution : it sets me grinning.

Eva.

Would we could end, and fly this arena !

Walter.

I only wish he 'd make a beginning.

(They follow the proceedings with increasing interest.)

Beckmesser

(who, while Sachs has continued his song and work, takes
counsel with himself in great perturbation).

Now if he continues I am undone !

(He advances to the shop.)

Friend Sachs ! pray hear a word — just one !
You work there at my shoes so fleetly,
While I 'd forgotten them completely.
The cobbler worshipful I deem ;
The critic, though, I more esteem.
Your taste, I know, is seldom wrong ;
So, please you, hear this little song,
With which I seek to win to-morrow :
Your estimate I fain would borrow.

(With his back turned to the alley he strums on the lute to
attract the attention of Magdalena and keep her at the
window.)

Sachs.

Aha ! A trap your words are holding !
But I 'll not earn another scolding.
Since that your cobbler courts the Muse
It fares but ill with your boots and shoes :
I see they 're slit :
And ev'rywhere split ;
So all my verse and rhyme
I 'll lay aside for a time,
My sense, my wit, my knowledge and all ;
Then with your new pair of shoes I 'll call.

Walther

(das Schwert halb ziehend).

Nun denn : mit dem Schwert !

Eva.

Nicht doch !   Ach halt' !

Walther.

Kaum wär' er's werth

Eva.

Ja, besser Geduld !   O lieber Mann !
Dass ich so Noth dir machen kann !

Walther.

Wer ist am Fenster ?

Eva.

's ist Magdalene.

Walther.

Das heiss' ich vergelten : fast muss' ich lachen.

Eva.

Wie ich ein End' und Flucht mir ersehne !

Walther.

Ich wünscht' er möchte den Anfang machen.

(Sie folgen dem Vorgang mit wachsender Theilnahme.)

Beckmesser

(der, während Sachs fortfährt zu arbeiten und zu singen, in
grosser Aufregung mit sich berathen hat).

Jetzt bin ich verloren, singt er noch fort !

(Er tritt an den Laden heran.)

Freund Sachs !   So hört doch nur ein Wort !
Wie seid ihr auf die Schuh' versessen !
Ich hatt' sie wahrlich schon vergessen.
Als Schuster seid ihr mir wohl werth,
Als Kunstfreund doch weit mehr verehrt.
Eu'r Urtheil, glaubt, das halt' ich hoch ;
D'rum bitt' ich, hört das Liedlein doch,
Mit dem ich morgen möcht' gewinnen,
Ob das auch recht nach euren Sinnen.

Er klimpert, mit seinem Rücken der Gasse zugewendet
auf der Laute, um die Aufmerksamkeit der dort am Fenster
sich zeigenden Magdalene zu beschäftigen, und sie dadurch
zurückzuhalten.

Sachs.

O ha !   Wollt mich beim Wahne fassen !
Mag mich nicht wieder schelten lassen.
Seit sich der Schuster dünkt Poet,
Gar übel es um eu'r Schuhwerk steht ;
Ich seh' wie's schlappt,
Und überall klappt :
D'rum lass' ich Vers' und Reim'
Gar billig nun daheim,
Verstand und Kenntniss auch dazu,
Mach' euch für morgen die neuen Schuh'.

Beckmesser.

Atrocious malice ! — Zounds ! it grows late !
She 'll go from the window if longer I wait !

(He strums a prelude.)

Sachs

(with a blow of his hammer).

" Now begin " !   Look sharp, or I too shall sing !

Beckmesser.

Aught but that !   Pray hush ! — What a madd'ning
thing !
Would you the post of Marker aspire to,
Then hammer away as you desire to : —
But you must agree to restrain your tool ;
Not strike unless I 'm breaking a rule.

Sachs.

Though a cobbler I 'll keep the rules like you,
If my fingers itch to complete this shoe.

Beckmesser.

Your Master's word ?

Sachs.

And cobbler's truth.

Beckmesser.

If it is faultless, fair, and smooth —

Sachs.

Then you must go unshod, forsooth !
Sit you down here !

Beckmesser

(placing himself at the corner of the house).

I 'd rather leave you.

Sachs.

Why so far off ?

Beckmesser.

Not to perceive you :
The Marker in school hides in his place.

Sachs.

But I shall scarce hear you.

Beckmesser.

My pow'rful bass
Will not then stun you with its din.

Sachs.

That 's good ! — All right then ! — " Now begin " !

(Short prelude on the lute by Beckmesser, during which
Magdalena leans out of the window.)

Beckmesser.

Verdammte Bosheit ! — Gott, und 's wird spät :
Am End' mirdie Jungfervom Fenstergeht !

(Er klimpert wie um anzufangen.)

Sachs

(aufschlagend).

Fanget an ! 's pressirt !   Sonst sing' ich für mich !

Beckmesser.

Haltet ein !   Nur das nicht ! — Teufel ; wie ärger-
lich !
Wollt ihr euch denn als Merker erdreisten,
Nun gut, so merkt mit dém Hammer auf dem
Leisten ; —
Nur mit dem Beding, nach den Regeln scharf :
Aber nichts, was nach den Regeln ich darf.

Sachs.

Nach den Regeln, wie sie der Schuster kennt,
Dem die Arbeit unter den Händen brennt.

Beckmesser.

Auf Meister-Ehr' !

Sachs.

Und Schuster-Muth !

Beckmesser.

Nicht einen Fehler : glatt und gut !

Sachs.

Dann ging't ihr morgen unbeschuht. —
Setzt euch denn hier !

Beckmesser

(an die Ecke des Hauses sich stellend).

Lasst hier mich stehen !

Sachs.

Warum so fern ?

Beckmesser.

Euch nicht zu sehen,
Wie's Brauch in der Schul' vor dem Gemerk.

Sachs.

Da hör' ich euch echlecht !

Beckmesser.

Der Stimme Stärk'
Ich so gar lieblich dämpfen kann.

Sachs.

Wie fein ! — Nun gut denn ! — Fanget an !

(Kurzes Vorspiel Beckmesser's auf der Laute, wozu Magdalene sich breit in das Fenster legt.)

Walter
(to Eva).

What crazy sounds ! 'T is like a dream:
Still in the Singer's seat I seem.

Eva.

Sleep steals upon me like a spell.
For good or evil, who can tell?

(She sinks, as if stupefied, on Walter's breast. In this position they remain.)

Beckmesser
(with his lute).

  "I see the dawning daylight,
    With great plea*sure* I do.

(Sachs knocks. — Beckmesser starts but continues.)

        "For now my breast takes *a* right
          Courage both fresh and " —

(Sachs has dealt two blows. Beckmesser turns round softly
but in anger.)

      Is this a jest?
      What d' ye find bad there?

Sachs.

      Better have had there,
      "For now my breast
    Takes a right courage fresh and " —

Beckmesser.

      How would that lay right
      To rhyme with my "daylight"?

Sachs.

The melody do you think no matter?
Both words and notes should fit in song.

Beckmesser.

Absurd discussion ! — Leave off that clatter !
Or is it a plot?

Sachs.
      Oh, get along !

Beckmesser.

I 'm quite upset !

Sachs.
            Begin it once more,
And three bars rest meanwhile I 'll score.

Beckmesser
(aside).

'T is better that no attention I pay : —
If only she is not scared away !

      (He clears his throat and begins again.)

  "I see the dawning daylight,
    With great plea*sure* I do ;

Walther
(zu Eva).

Welch' toller Spuck ! Mich dünkt's ein Traum:
Den Singstuhl, scheint's, verliess ich kaum !

Eva.

Die Schläf' umwebt's mir, wie ein Wahn:
Ob's Heil, ob Unheil, was ich ahn'?

(Sie sinkt wie betäubt an Walther's Brust: so verblieben
sie.)

Beckmesser
(zur Laute).

  „Den Tag seh' ich erscheinen,
    Der mir wohl gefall'n thut. . .
        (Sachs schlägt auf.)
        (Beckmesser zuckt, fährt aber fort:)
  „ Da fasst mein Herz sich' einen
    guten und frischen Muth."

(Sachs hat zweimal aufgeschlagen. Beckmesser wendet
sich leise doch wüthend um.)

      Treibt ihr hier Scherz?
      Was wär' nicht gelungen?

Sachs.

      Besser gesungen :
      „ Da fasst mein Herz
    sich einen guten und frischen Muth."

Beckmesser.

      Wie sollt' sich das reimen
      Auf „ seh' ich erscheinen? "

Sachs.

Ist euch an der Weise nichts gelegen?
Mich dünkt, 'sollt' passen Ton und Wort.

Beckmesser.

Mit euch hier zu streiten? — Lasst von den Schlä-
                                            gen,
Sonst denkt ihr mir d'ran !

Sachs.
                  Jetzt fahret fort !

Beckmesser.

Bin ganz verwirrt !

Sachs.
            So fangt noch 'mal an :
Drei Schläg' ich jetzt pausiren kann.

Beckmesser
(für sich).

Am Besten, wenn ich ihn gar nicht beacht' : —
Wenn's nur die Jungfrau nicht irre macht !

      (Er räuspert sich und beginnt wieder.)

  „Den Tag seh' ich erscheinen,
    Der mir wohl gefall'n thut ;

For now my heart takes a right
Courage both fresh and new.
I do not think of dying,
Rather of trying
A young maiden to win.
Oh, wherefore doth the weather
Then to-day so excel?
I to all say together
'T is because a damsel
By her beloved father,
At his wish rather,
To be wed doth go in.
The bold man who
Would come and view,
May see the maiden there so true,
On whom my hopes I firmly glue:
Therefore is the sky so bright blue,
As I said to begin."

Beckmesser, keeping his eyes fixed on the window has perceived with rising chagrin Magdalena's evident signs of dissatisfaction; he has sung louder and more hurriedly in order to overpower the continued hammering of Sachs.— He is about to continue when the latter, knocking the key of the last out and withdrawing the shoes, rises from his stool and leans out over the shopdoor.

Sachs.

Have n't you finished?

Beckmesser

(in great trepidation).
What means your call?

Sachs

(triumphantly holding out the shoes from the door).

I 've finished with the shoes, that's all !—
I call that a famous Marker's shoe:
Now hear my Marker's maxim too.—
By long and short strokes dinted
Here on the sole 'tis printed !
Behold it here,
Let it be clear,
And hold it ever dear.—
"Good songs must scan."
On any man,
Ev'n the Town-clerk, who'd transgress it
The cobbler's strap shall impress it.—
Now run along,
Your shoes are strong;
Thrust henceforth to your feet:
They 'll keep you on the beat.

(He laughs loudly.)

Beckmesser

(who has retired into the alley again and leaned against the wall between Sachs's two windows, hastens on with his third verse, shouting breathlessly with violent efforts to drown Sachs's voice).

Da fasst mein Herz sich einen
Guten und frischen Muth.
Da denk' ich nicht an Sterben,
Lieber an Werben
Um jung' Mägdeleins Hand.
Warum wohl aller Tage
Schönster mag dieser sein?
Allen hier ich es sage:
Weil ein schönes Fräulein,
Von ihrem lieb'n Herrn Vater,
Wie gelobt hat er,
Ist bestimmt zum Eh' stand.
Wer sich getrau',
Der komm' und schau'
Da steh'n die hold lieblich Jungfrau,
Auf die ich all' mein' Hoffnung bau',
D'rum ist der Tag so schön blau,
Als ich anfänglich fand."

Beckmesser, nur den Blick auf das Fenster heftend, hat mit wachsender Angst Magdalene's missbehagliche Gebärden bemerkt; um Sachsen's fortgesetzte Schläge zu übertäuben, hat er immer stärker und athemloser gesungen.— Er ist im Begriffe sofort weiter zu singen, als Sachs, der zuletzt die Kelle aus den Leisten schlug, und die Schuhe abgezogen hat, sich vom Schemel erhebt, und über den Laden sich herauslehnt.

Sachs.

Seid ihr nun fertig?

Beckmesser

(in höchster Angst).
Wie fraget ihr?

Sachs

(die Schuhe triumphirend aus dem Laden heraushaltend).

Mit den Schuhen ward' ich fertig schier!
Das heiss' ich mir rechte Merkerschuh';
Mein Merkersprüchlein hört dazu !
Mit lang' und kurzen Hieben,
Steht's auf der Sohl' geschrieben:
Da les't es klar
Und nehmt es wahr,
Und merkt's euch immerdar.—
Gut Lied will Takt,
Wer den verzwackt,
Dem Schreiber mit der Feder
Haut ihn der Schuster auf's Leder.
Nun lauft iu Ruh',
Habt gute Schuh';
Der Fuss euch d'rin nicht knackt:
Ihn hält die Sohl' im Takt !

(Er lacht laut.)

Beckmesser

(der sich ganz in die Gasse zurückgezogen, und an die Mauer zwischen den beiden Fenstern von Sachsens Hause sich anlehnt, singt, um Sachs zu übertäuben, zugleich, mit grösster Anstrengung, schreiend und athemlos hastig, seinen dritten Vers).

That I 've a Master's learning
Willingly I 'd show her,
To win the *reward* burning
I 'm *with* thirst *and* hunger.
Now I call *the* nine Muses
To witness whose is
The *poetic* gift true.
I lay no faulty stresses,
In *the* rules I 'm no dunce ;
Some little awkwardnesses
May *excused* be for once,
When *one's* heart fear is swaying
At thus essaying
A fair maid*en* to woo.
A bachelor.
I 'd give my gore,
My place, rank, honor, all my store,
If *you* my song would not abhor ;
And *the* maid*en* would me adore
If she admires it too."

Neighbors

(first a few, then more, open their windows in the alley during the song and peep out).

Who 's howling there ?   Who bawls so loud ?
So late at night, is that allowed ?
'T is time for bed !   Be still, I say !
Just listen to that donkey's bray !
You there !   Shut up and beat retreat !
Go halloa in some other street !

David

(who has opened his shutter close to Beckmesser).

Whoever 's this, and who 's up there ?
'T is Magdalena, I declare !
'Oddzounds ! that 's it — I clearly see
'T is he she favors more than me !
You 'll catch it !   Just wait !   I 'll tan your skin !
The devil help you when I begin !

(David, arming himself with a cudgel, springs out of the window, knocks Beckmesser's lute out of his hands and throws himself upon him.)

Magdalena

(who at last, to make the Marker go, has made exaggerated gestures of pleasure at him, now cries aloud).

O heavens !   David !   Lord, how I 'm thrilled !
A rescue ! a rescue ! or both will be killed !

Beckmesser
(struggling with David).

Infernal rogue !   Let me alone !

David.

I will when I 've broken every bone.
(They continue to struggle and fight.)

„ Darf ich Meister mich nennen,
Das bewähr' ich heut gern,
Weil nach dem Preis ich brenne
Muss dursten und hungern,
Nun ruf' ich die neun Musen,
Dass an sie blusen
Mein dichtr'schen Verstand.
Wohl kenn' ich alle Regeln,
Halte gut Mass und Zahl ;
Doch Sprung und Ueberkegeln
Wohl passirt je einmal,
Wann der Kopf, ganz voll Zagen,
Zu frei'n will wagen
Um ein jung' Mägdleins Hand.
Ein Junggesell,
Trug ich mein Fell,
Mein Ehr', Amt, Würd' und Brod zur Stell',
Dass euch mein Gesang wohl gefäll',
Und mich das Jungfräulein erwähl',
Wenn sie mein Lied gut fand."

Nachbarn

(erst einige, dann mehrere, öffnen während des Gesanges in der Gasse die Fenster und gucken heraus).

Wer heult denn da !. Wer kreischt mit Macht ?
Ist das erlaubt, so spät zur Nacht ?—
Gebt Ruhe hier ! 's ist Schlafenszeit !—
Nein, hört nur, wie der Esel schreit !—
Ihr da !   Seid still, und scheert euch fort !
Heult, kreischt und schreit an and'rem Ort !

David

(hat ebenfalls den Fensterladen, dicht bei Beckmesser, ein wenig geöffnet und lugt hervor).

Wer Teufel hier ?— Und drüben gar ?
Die Lene ist's, — ich seh' es klar !
Herr Je ! das war's, den hat sie bestellt ;
Der ist's, der ihr besser als ich gefällt !—
Nun warte ! du kriegt's ! dir streich' ich das Fell !—
Zum Teufel mit dir, verdammter Gesell' !

(David ist, mit einem Knüpple bewaffnet, hinter dem Laden aus dem Fenster hervorgesprungen, zerschlägt Beckmesser's Laute und wirft sich über ihn selbst her.)

Magdalene

(die zuletzt, um den Merker zu entfernen, mit übertriebenen Beifälligen Bewegungen herabgewinkt hat, schreit jetzt laut auf).

Ach Himmel !   David !   Gott, welche Noth !
Zu Hülfe ! zu Hülfe !   Sie schlagen sich todt !

Beckmesser
(mit David sich balgend).

Verfluchter Kerl !   Lässt du mich los ?

David.

Gewiss !   Die Glieder brech' ich dir blos !
(Sie balgen und prügeln sich in einem fort.)

Neighbors
(at the windows).

Look there! Go to! They're hard at it now!

Other Neighbors
(coming into the alley).

Hallo? What's up? See, here's a row!
You there! stand back! Give him fair play!
If you don't part we'll join the fray.

One Neighbor.

Halloa? Have you come? Why are you here?

A Second.

What's that to you! Don't interfere!

First Neighbor.

You're a big rogue!

Second Neighbor.

You are no lesser!

First Neighbor.

Prove it, then!

Second Neighbor
(hitting out).

There!

Magdalena
(screaming down).

David! Beckmesser!

Prentices
(entering).

Hooray! hooray! Here's cudgel play!

Some.

It's the cobblers!

Others.

No, it's the tailors!

The First.

The drunken patches!

The Others.

The starveling railers!

The Neighbors
(in the street, to one another).

That pays what I owe you! —
Coward! I know you! —
Take that to requite you! —
Mind your eye if I smite you! —
Was your wife's temper high? —
See how the cudgels fly! —
Have n't you found your wits? —
Lay on, then! — Toat hits!

Nachbarn
(an den Fenstern).

Seht nach! Springt zu! Da würgen sich zwei!

Andere Nachbarn
(auf die Gasse heraustretend).

Heda, Herbei! 's gibt Prügelei!
Ihr da! auseinander! Gebt freien Lauf!
Lasst ihr nicht los, wir schlagen drauf!

Ein Nachbar.

Ei seht! Auch ihr da? Geht's euch 'was an?

Ein Zweiter.

Was sucht ihr hier? Hat man euch 'was gethan?

Erster Nachbar.

Euch kennt man gut!

Zweiter Nachbar.

Euch noch viel besser!

Erster Nachbar.

Wie so denn?

Zweiter Nachbar
(zuschlagend).

Ei, so!

Magdalene
(hinabschreiend).

David! Beckmesser!

Lehrbuben
(kommen dazu).

Herbei! Herbei! 's gibt Keilerei!

Einige.

's sind die Schuster!

Andere.

Nein, 's sind die Schneider!

Die Ersteren.

Die Trunkenbolde!

Die Anderen.

Die Hungerleider!

Die Nachbarn.
(auf der Gasse, durcheinander).

Euch gönnt ich's schon lange! —
Wird euch wohl bange?
Das für die Klage! —
Seht euch vor, wenn ich schlage! —
Hat euch die Frau gehetzt? —
Schau' wie es Prügel setzt! —
Seid ihr noch nicht gewitzt!
So schlagt doch! — Das sitzt! —

Rogue, there 's a thumper !—
You counter-jumper !—
You gutter-sweeper !—
You false-measure-keeper !
Blockhead ! — Looby !—
You great Booby !—
Dolt, I say !
Don't give way !

Prentices

(to one another, with the neighbors).

We know the locksmiths' way :
They surely started this fray !—
I think the smiths began the fight. —
I see the joiners by the light. —
Look where the coopers come along !
And now the barbers join the throng. —
There the Guild of grocers comes,
With lollipops and sugarplums,
With pepper, spice, and cinnamon.
 How nice they smell !
 How nice they smell !
But they don't like the fun,
And wish that it were done.
 See that fool there,
 With his nose ev'rywhere !
Pray did you allude to me ?—
Pray did I allude to thee ?
There 's one nose I 've pounded !—
Lord ! how that sounded !—
Hey ! whack ! fire and fury oh !
Where that fell no hair will grow !
 Cudgels, whack hard !
 Smash the blackguard !
Show yourselves worth freemen's name :
To give way would be a shame !
 Join the brawl,
 Each and all.
We are ready to help the row !

(Gradually the neighbors and Prentices have come to a
  general fight.)

Journeymen

(arriving from all quarters).

Hallo ! Companions, come !
The people here seem quarrelsome.
There 'll surely be some fighting then :
Be ready, lusty journeymen.
'T is the weaver and tanners !—
Which well I know !—
'T is like their manners !—
They always do so !—
Klaus the butcher 's there ;
He 's one to beware !—
Guilds ! Guilds !
Guilds ! ev'rywhere !—

Dass dich, Hallunke !—
Hie Färbertunke !—
Wartet, ihr Racker !
Ihr Maassabzwacker !—
Esel ! — Dummrian !—
Du Grobian !—
Lümmel du !—
Drauf und zu !

Lehrbuben

(durcheinander, zugleich mit den Nachbarn).

Kennt man die Schlosser nicht ?
Die haben's sicher angericht' !
Ich glaub' die Schmiede werden's sein. —
Die Schreiner seh' ich dort beim Schein.
Hei ! Schau' die Schäffler dort beim Tanz.
Dort seh' die Bader ich im Glanz. —
Krämer finden sich zur Hand
Mit Gerstenstang und Zuckerkand ;
Mit Pfeffer, Zimmt, Muscatennuss,
 Sie riechen schön,
 Sie riechen schön,
Doch haben viel Verdruss,
Und bleiben gern vom Schuss. —
 Seht nur, der Hase
Hat üb'rall die Nase !
Meinst du damit etwa mich !—
Mein' ich damit etwa dich ?
Da hast's auf die Schnautze !—
Herr, jetzt setzt's Plautze !—
Hei ! Krach ! Hagelwetterschlag !
Wo das sitzt, da wächst nichts nach :
 Keilt euch wacker,
Haut die Racker !
Haltet selbst Gesellen Stand ;
Wer da wich', 's wär' wahrlich Schand' !
 Drauf und dran !
 Wie ein Mann
Steh'n wir alle zur Keilerei !

(Bereits prügeln sich Nachbarn und Lehrbuben fast allgemein durcheinander.)

Gesellen

(von allen Seiten dazu kommend).

Heda ! Gesellen 'ran !
Dort wird mit Streit und Zank gethan,
Da giebt's gewiss gleich Schlägerei ;
Gesellen, haltet euch dabei !
'Sind die Weber und Gerber !—
Dacht' ich's doch gleich !—
Die Preisverderber !
Spielen immer Streich' !—
Dort den Metzger Klaus,
Den kennt man heraus !—
Zünfte ! Zünfte !
Zünfte heraus !—

Tailors here are hieing!—
See the cudgels flying!
Girdlers!— Pewterers!
Glue-boilers!— Fruiterers!
Clothworkers here!
Linenweavers here!
Come here! Come here!
More appear! More appear!
All do your best! We're going to strike!
Now will the fight be something like!—
Run home! your wife is after you!
Here you'll get painted black and blue!
  There they go!
  Blow for blow!
  Knock them over!
Guildsmen! Guildsmen! come out!

The Masters

  (and old Burghers arriving on all sides).

What is this noise of brawl and fight,
That sounds far through the night?
Leave off and let each go his way,
Or else there'll be the deuce to pay!
Don't crowd up like this in bands,
Or else we too must use our hands.

Women

  (at the windows to one another).

What is this noise of fight and brawl?
It really terrifies us all!
My husband's there, as sure as fate!
Some one will get a broken pate!
  Hey, sirs! You below there,
  Be reasonable now!
  Are you then all so ready
  To join a vulgar row?
  What a confusion and halloa!
  Now blows will be certain to follow!
  Hark ye! hark ye!
  Are ye insane?
  Are ye still fuddled
  With wine on the brain?
  O murder! murder!
  My man's in the fight!
  There's father! there's father!
  Look! what a sight!
  Christian! Peter!
  Nicholas! Hans!
  Watch! be fleeter!—
  Don't you hear, Franz?
  Lord! how the hair flies!
  See how they go it!
  Water here! Water, quick!
  On their heads throw it!

(The row has become general. Shrieks and blows.)

Schneider mit dem Bügei!
Hei! hie setzt's Prügel!
Gürtler!— Zinngiesser!—
Leimsieder!— Lichtgiesser!—
Tuchscherer her!
Leinweber her!
Hierher! Hierher!
Immer mehr! Immer mehr
Nur tüchtig drauf! Wir schlagen los
Jetzt wird die Keilerei erst gross!—
Lauft heim, sonst kriegt ihr's von der Frau,
Hier giebt's nur Prügel-Färberblau!
  Immer 'ran!
  Mann für Mann!
  Schlagt sie nieder!
Zünfte! Zünfte! Heraus!—

Die Meister

  (und älteren Bürger von verschiedenen Seiten dazu
    kommend).

Was giebt's denn da für Zank und Streit?
Das tos't ja weit und breit!
Gebt Ruh' und scheer' sich jeder heim!
Sonst schlag' ein Hageldonnerwetter drein!
Stemmt euch hier nicht mehr zu Hauf,
Oder sonst wir schlagen krauf.—

Die Nachbarinnen

  (an den Fenstern, durcheinander).

Was ist denn da für Streit und Zank?
's wird einem wahrlich angst und bang!
Da ist mein Mann gewiss dabei:
Gewiss kommt's noch zur Schlägerei!
  He da! Ihr dort unten,
  So seid doch nur gescheit!
  Seid ihr zu Streit und Raufen
  Gleich Alle so bereit?
  Was für ein Zanken und Toben!
  Da werden schon Arme erhoben,
  Hört doch! Hört doch!
  Seid ihr denn toll?
  Sind euch die Köpfe
  Vom Weine noch voll?
  Zu Hülfe! Zu Hülfe!
  Da schlägt sich mein Mann!
  Der Vater! Der Vater!
  Sieht man das an?
  Christian! Peter!
  Nikolaus! Hans!
  Auf! schrei't Zeter!—
  Hörst du nicht, Franz?
  Gott, wie sie walken!
  's wackeln die Zöpfe!
  Wasser her! Wasser her!
  Giesst's ihn' auf die Köpfe!

(Die Rauferei ist allgemein. Schreien und Toben.)

Magdalena

(wringing her hands despairingly at the window).

Oh heaven! what is to be done!
David, for goodness' sake attend!
Do leave the gentleman alone!

Pogner

(coming to the window in his nightgown, pulls Magdalena in).

Come in, Eva! Odd so!
I'll see if all is right below.

The window is shut and Pogner appears below at the door.

Sachs at the commencement of the row has extinguished his light and set his door ajar, so as still to be able to watch the place under the lime-tree.

(Walter and Eva have observed the riot with increasing anxiety. Now Walter seizes Eva in his arms.)

Walter.

Now we may do it —
Cut our way through it!

Brandishing his sword he forces a way to the middle of the stage.— Sachs rushes with one bound out of his shop and grasps Walter's arms.

Pogner

(on the steps).

Ho! Lena! where are you?

Sachs

(pushing the half-fainting Eva up the steps).

Go in, Mistress Lena!

Pogner receives her and pulls her within.

Sachs brandishing his knee-strap, with which he has cleared a path to Walter, now catches David one, and kicking him into the shop, drags Walter, whom he still holds, indoors with him, closing and barring the door behind them.

Beckmesser, released from David by Sachs, seeks hasty flight through the crowd.

At the moment Sachs rushes into the street a loud note from the Nightwatchman's horn is heard R. U. E. Prentices, Burghers, and Journeymen, panic-struck, seek flight on all sides, so that the stage is speedily completely cleared: all doors are closed and women gone from windows, which are also shut.— The full moon shines out and brightly illumines the now peaceful alley.

The Watchman

(enters R. U. E., rubs his eyes, stares about him in surprise, shakes his head, and in a somewhat tremulous voice calls out):

"Hark to what I say, good people!
Eleven strikes from every steeple;
Defend you all from spectre and sprite,
Let no power of ill your souls affright.
            Praise the Lord of Heaven."

He goes slowly up the alley. As the curtain falls his distant horn is still heard.

Magdalene

(am Fenster verzweifelt die Hände ringend).

Ach Himmel! Meine Noth ist gross!—
David! So hör, mich doch nur an!
So lass' doch nur den Herrn los!

Pogner

(ist im Nachtgewand oben an das Fenster getreten and zieht Magdalene herein).

Um Gott! Eva! schliess' zu!
Ich seh', ob im Haus unten Ruh'!

Das Fenster wird geschlossen; bald darauf erscheint Pogner an der Hausthüre.

Sachs hat, als der Tumult begann, sein Licht gelöscht und den Laden so weit geschlossen, dass er durch eine kleine Oeffnung stets den Platz unter der Linde beobachten kann.

Walther und Eva haben mit wachsender Sorge dem anschwellenden Tumult zugesehen. Jetzt fasst Walther Eva dicht in den Arm.

Walther.

Jetzt gilt's zu wagen,
Sich durchzuschlagen!

Mit geschwungenem Schwerte dringt er bis in die Mitte der Bühne vor. — Da springt Sachs mit einem Satz aus dem Laden auf die Strasse, und packt Walther beim Arm.

Pogner

(auf der Treppe).

He, Lene, wo bist du?

Sachs

(die halb ohnmächtige Eva auf die Treppe stossend).

In's Haus, Jungfer Lene!

Pogner empfängt sie, und zieht sie beim Arme herein.

Sachs mit dem geschwungenen Knieriemen, mit dem er sich bereits bis zu Walther Platz gemacht hatte, jetzt dem David eines überhauend, und ihn mit einem Fusstritt voran in den Laden stossend, zieht Walther, den er mit der andern Hand gefasst hält, gewaltsam schnell mit sich ebenfalls hinein, und schliesst sogleich fest hinter sich zu.

Beckmesser, durch Sachs von David befreit, sucht sich eilig durch die Menge zu flüchten.

Im gleichen Augenblicke, wo Sachs auf die Strasse sprang, hörte man, rechts zur Seite im Vordergrunde, einen besonders starken Hornruf des Nachtwächters. Lehrbuben, Bürger und Gesellen suchten in eiliger Flucht sich nach allen Seiten hin zu entfernen, so dass die Bühne sehr schnell gänzlich geleert ist, alle Hausthüren hastig geschlossen, und auch die Nachbarinnen von den Fenstern, welche sie zugeschlagen, verschwunden sind — Der Vollmond tritt hervor und scheint hell in die Gasse hinein.

Der Nachtwächter

(betritt im Vordergrunde rechts die Bühne, reibt sich die Augen, sieht sich verwundert um, schüttelt den Kopf, und stimmt, mit etwas bebender Stimme, seinen Ruf an):

Hört ihr Leut', und lasst euch sagen:
Die Glock' hat Eilfe geschlagen,
Bewahrt euch vor Gespenstern und Spuck,
Dass kein böser Geist eur' Seel' beruck'!
            Lobet Gott den Herrn!

Er geht währenddem langsam die Gasse hinab. Als der Vorhang fällt, hört man den Hornruf des Nachtwächters wiederholen.

THIRD ACT.

In Sachs's workshop. (Front scene.) At back the half-open shopdoor leads to the street. R. the door of a chamber. L. the window looking into the alley, flowers in pots before it; a workbench beside it. Sachs sits at this window in a great armchair, the bright morning sun streaming in on him; he has a large folio on his lap and is absorbed in reading. — David peeps in at the door from the street; on seeing that Sachs does not notice him he enters with a basket on his arm, which he first hides quickly under the other workbench; then again assured that Sachs does not heed him, he carefully takes it out again and investigates the contents: he lifts out flowers and ribbons and at last finds at the bottom a sausage and a cake; these he is about to devour when Sachs, who is still unconscious of his presence, turns over a leaf of his book with a loud rustle.

David

(starts, hides the eatables, and turns round).

Here, Master! Yes! —
The shoes were taken duly
To clerk Beckmesser's address.
I thought you summoned me, truly.

(Aside.)

He seems to notice me not!
When he is dumb his anger 's hot.

(Gradually approaching humbly.)

Ah, Master! won't you forgive?
Can a Prentice quite faultless live?
If with my eyes Lena you 'd see
You 'd pardon me assuredly.
She is so good, so kind to me,
And eyes me at times so tenderly.
When I 've been thrashed soothing is she
And smiles upon me so prettily!
When on short commons she feedeth me,
And acts in all things right lovingly.
Last night, though, when that knight was discarded,
There was no basket to me awarded:
That worried me, and when I found
At night when some one lurked around,
And sang to her and cried like mad,
I gave him all the stick I had.
What dreadful consequence befell!
But yet for our love it turned out well;
Now Lena 's explained the matter to me,
And sent all these ribbons and flowers you see.

(He bursts out in still greater anxiety.)

O Master! speak one word I pray!

(Aside.)

Would I 'd put the cake and sausage away!

DRITTER AUFZUG.

In Sachsen's Werkstatt. (Kurzer Raum.) Im Hintergrund die halb geöffnete Ladenthüre, nach der Strasse führend. Rechts zur Seite eine Kammerthüre. Links das nach der Gasse gehende Fenster, mit Blumenstöcken davor, zur Seite ein Werktisch. Sachs sitzt auf einem grossen Lehnstuhle an diesem Fenster, durch welches die Morgensonne hell auf ihn hereinscheint; er hat vor sich auf dem Schoose einen grossen Folianten und ist im Lesen vertieft. — David lugt spähend von der Strasse zur Ladenthüre herein: da er sieht, dass Sachs seiner nicht achtet, tritt er herein, mit einem Korbe im Arm, den er zuvörderst schnell und verstohlen unter den andern Werktisch beim Laden stellt; — dann von neuem versichert, dass Sachs ihn nicht bemerkt, nimmt er den Korb vorsichtig herauf, und untersucht den Inhalt; er hebt Blumen und Bänder heraus; endlich findet er auf dem Grunde eine Wurst und einen Kuchen, und lässt sich sogleich an, diese zu verzehren, als Sachs, der ihn fortwährend nicht beachtet, mit starkem Geräusch eines der grossen Blätter des Folianten unwendet.

David

(fährt zusammen, verbirgt das Essen und wendet sich).

Gleich! Meister! Hier! —
Die Schuh' sind abgegeben
In Herrn Beckmesser's Quartier. —
Mir war's, ihr rief't mich eben?

(Bei Seite.)

Er thut, als säh' er mich nicht?
Da ist er bös', wenn er nicht spricht!

(Sich demüthig sehr allmählich nähernd.)

Ach Meister wollt ihr mir verzeih'n!
Kann ein Lehrbub' vollkommen sein?
Kenntet ihr die Lene, wie ich,
Da vergäbt ihr mir sicherlich.
Sie ist so gut, so sanft für mich,
Und blickt mich oft an, so innerlich:
Wenn ihr mich schlagt, streichelt sie mich,
Und lächelt dabei holdseliglich!
Muss ich cariren, füttert sie mich,
Und ist in Allem gar liebelich.
Nur gestern, weil der Junker versungen,
Hab' ich den Korb ihr nicht abgerungen:
Das schmerzte mich; und da ich fand,
Dass Nachts Einer vor dem Fenster stand,
Und sang zu ihr, und schrie wie toll,
Da hieb ich dem den Buckel voll.
Wie käm' nun da 'was Gross' drauf an?
Auch hat's uns'rer Lieb' gar gut gethan:
Die Lene hat eben mir Alles erklärt,
Und zum Fest Blumen und Bänder bescheert,

(Er bricht in immer grössere Angst aus.)

Ach, Meister, sprecht doch nur ein Wort!

(Bei Seite.)

Hätt' ich nur die Wurst und den Kuchen fort.

Sachs

(who has read on undisturbed, claps his book to. At the loud noise David is so startled that he stumbles and falls unintentionally on his knees before Sachs. The latter gazes far away beyond the book which he still holds, beyond David who, from his kneeling posture looks up at him in terror, and his eyes fall on the farther table).

Yonder are flowers and ribbons gay
In youthful beauty and bloom :
How came they into my room?

David

(astonished at Sachs's friendliness).

Why, Master ! to-day 's a feast, you know,
And all must smarten to grace the show.

Sachs.

Is 't a marriage feast?

David.

Yea, so it would be
If only Lena might marry me.

Sachs.

Your Folly-evening* was last night?

David

(aside).

Folly-evening? — I 'm all in a fright !

(Aloud.)

Forgive me, Master ! Forget it, pray !
The Feast of St. John we keep to-day.

Sachs.

St. John's day?

David

(aside).

Deaf he must be !

Sachs.

Know you your verses? Repeat them me.

David.

My verses? Yes, they 're in my brain. —

(Aside.)

All right ! the master is kind again ! —

(Aloud.)

"St. John stood on the Jordan's strand" —

(In his agitation he sings his lines to the melody of Beckmesser's serenade; he is pulled up by Sachs's movement of astonishment.)

Forgive me, master, and pardon the slip !
That Folly-evening caused me to trip.

* "Polterabend" — the merrymaking on the eve of a German wedding.

Sachs

(der unbeirrt weiter gelesen, schlägt jetzt den Folianten zu. Von dem starken Geräusch erschrickt David so, dass er strauchelt und unwillkürlich vor Sachs auf die Knie fällt. Sachs sieht über das Buch, das er noch auf dem Schoosse behält, hinweg, über David, welcher immer auf den Knieen, furchtsam nach ihm hinauf blickt, hin, und heftet seinen Blick unwillkürlich auf den hintern Werktisch).

Blumen und Bänder seh' ich dort : —
Schaut hold und jugendlich aus !
Wie kamen die mir in's Haus?

David

(verwundert über Sachsens Freundlichkeit).

Ei, Meister? 's is heut' hoch festlicher Tag ;
Da putzt sich jeder, so schön er mag.

Sachs.

Wär' Hochzeitsfest?

David.

Ja, käm's so weit,
Dass David erst die Lene freit !

Sachs.

's war Polterabend dünkt mich 'doch?

David

(für sich).

Polterabend? — Da krieg ich's wohl noch ! —

(Laut.)

Verzeiht das, Meister ! Ich bitt', vergesst,
Wir feiern ja heut' Johannisfest.

Sachs.

Johannisfest?

David

(bei Seite).

Hört er heut' schwer?

Sachs.

Kannst du ein Sprüchlein? Sag' es her !

David.

Mein Sprüchlein? Denk', ich kann es gut.

(Bei Seite.)

'Setzt nichts ! der Meister ist wohlgemuth ! —

(Laut.)

„ Am Jordan Sankt Johannes stand " —

(Er hat in der Zerstreuung die Worte mit der Melodie von Beckmesser's Werbelied aus dem vorhergehenden Aufzuge gesungen; Sachs macht eine verwundernde Bewegung, worauf David sich unterbricht.)

Verzeiht, Meister ; ich kam in's Gewirr :
Der Polterabend machte mich irr.

(He recommences to the proper tune.)

"St. John stood on the Jordan's strand,
    Where all the world he christened:
A woman came from distant land,
    From Nuremberg she 'd hastened:
Her little son she led in hand,
    Baptized him with a name there,
And then toward home she took her flight;
    But when at last she came there
It soon turned out in German lands,
That he who on the Jordan's sands
    Johannes had been hight,
    On the Pegnitz was called Hans."

(Impetuously.)

Sir! Master! 'T is your name-day, sure!
There! Well, my memory must be poor!
Here! all the flowers are for you.
The ribbons — something else there was, too?
Yes, here! Look. Master! Here 's a fine pasty!
Try, too, this sausage, you 'll find it tasty.

Sachs

(still dreamily, without moving).

Best thanks, my lad! You keep it though!
Anon to the meadow with me you shall go.
With ribbons and flowers make yourself gay;
As my herald you are to act to-day.

David.

Would I not be your groomsman more fain?
Master, dear master! you *must* wed again!

Sachs.

Do you wish for a mistress then here?

David.

Methinks more dignified it would appear.

Sachs.

Who knows? But time will show.

David.

Time 's come.

Sachs.

Has it brought knowledge then to some?

David.

Aye, sure! I know things have been repeated;
And Beckmesser's singing you have defeated.
I think he will scarce make a stir to-day.

Sachs.

'T is likely! That I 'll not gainsay.
Now, go; disturb not Sir Walter's rest!
Come back when you are finely dress'd.

(Er fährt in der richtigen Melodie fort.)

„Am Jordan Sankt Johannes stand,
    All Volk der Welt zu taufen:
Kam auch ein Weib aus fremden Land,
    Von Nürnberg gar gelaufen;
Sein Söhnlein trug's zum Nferrand,
    Empfing da Tauf' und Namen;
Doch als sie dann sich heimgewandt,
    Nach Nürnberg wieder kamen,
Im deutschen Land gar bald sich fand's,
Dass, wer am Ufer des Jordans
    Johannes war genannt,
    An der Pegnitz hiess der Hans."

(Feurig.)

Herr Meister! 's ist eu'r Namenstag!
Nein! Wie man so 'was vergessen mag!
Hier! hier, die Blumen sind für euch,
Die Bänder, — und was nur Alles noch gleich?
Ja hier! schaut, Meister! Herrlicher Kuchen!
Möchtet ihr nicht auch die Wurst versuchen?

Sachs

(immer ruhig, ohne seine Stellung zu verändern).

Schön Dank, mein Jung'! behalt's für dich!
Doch heut' auf die Wiese' begleitest du mich:
Mit den Bändern und Blumen putz' dich fein;
Sollst mein stattlicher Herold sein.

David.

Sollt' ich nicht lieber Brautführer sein?
Meister! lieb' Meister! ihr müsst wieder frei'n!

Sachs.

Hätt'st wohl gern eine Meist'rin im Haus?

David.

Ich mein', es säh doch viel stattlicher aus.

Sachs.

Wer weiss! Kommt Zeit, kommt Rath.

David.

                              's ist Zeit!

Sachs.

Da wär' der Rath wohl auch nicht weit?

David.

Gewiss! geh'n die Reden schon hin und wieder.
Den Beckmesser, denk' ich säng't ihr doch nieder?
Ich mein', dass der heut' sich nicht wenig wichtig
                      macht.

Sachs.

Wohl möglich! Hab's mir auch schon bedacht
Jetzt geh'; doch stör' mir den Junker nicht!
Komm wieder, wenn du schön gericht'.

David

moved, kisses Sachs's hand, collects his things and goes
into chamber).

He ne'er was like this, though sometimes kind !
Why, the taste of his strap has gone out of my
mind !

(Exit.)

Sachs

(still with the book on his knees leans back deep in thought,
resting his head on his hand, and after a pause begins).

Mad !   Mad !
All the world 's mad !
Where'er enquiry dives
In town or world's archives
And seeks to learn the reason
Why people strive and fight,
Both in and out of season,
In fruitless rage and spite.
What do they gain
For all their pain?
Repulsed in fight,
They feign joy in flight ;
Their pain-cries not minding,
They joy pretend
When their own flesh their fingers rend,
And pleasure deem they 're finding.
What tongue the cause can phrase?
'T is just the same old craze !
Naught haps without it ever,
In spite of all endeavor,
Pause doth it make ;
In sleep it but acquires new force,
Soon it will wake,
Then, lo ! who can control its course?
Old ways and customs keeping,
How peacefully I see
My dear old Nurnberg sleeping
In midst of Germany !
But on one evening late,
To hinder in some fashion
The follies of youthful passion,
A man worries his pate ;
A shoemaker, all unknowing,
Sets the old madness going :
How soon from highways and alleys
A raging rabble sallies !
Man, woman, youth, and child
Blindly fall to as if gone wild ;
And ere the craze lose power
The cudgel blows must shower ;
They seek with fuss and pother
The fires of wrath to smother.
God knows how this befell !
'T was like some impish spell !
Some glowworm could not find his mate ;
'T was he aroused this wrath and hate.

David

(küsst ihm gerührt die Hand, packt Alles zusammen, und
geht in die Kammer).

So war er noch nie, wenn sonst auch gut !
Kann mir gar nicht mehr denken, wie der Knieriemen thut !

(Ab.)

Sachs

(immer noch den Folianten auf dem Schoose, lehnt sich,
mit untergestütztem Arme, sinnend darauf und beginnt
dann nach einem Schweigen).

Wahn !   Wahn !
Uberall !   Wahn !
Wohin ich forschend blick',
In Stadt- und Welt-Chronik,
Den Grund mir aufuzufinden,
Warum gar bis auf's Blut
Die Leut' sich quälen und schinden
In unnütz toller Wuth !
Hat keiner Lohn
Noch dank davon :
In Flucht geschlagen,
Meint er zu jagen.
Hört nicht sein eigen
Schmerz Gekreisch,
Wenn er sich wühlt in's eig'ne Fleisch
Wähnt Lust sich zu erzeigen.
Wer giebt den Namen an !
's bleibt halt der alte Wahn,
Ohn' den nichts mag geschehen,
's mag gehen oder stehen !
Steht's wo im Lauf,
Er schläft nur neue Kraft sich an ; .
Gleich wacht er auf,
Dann schaut wer ihn bemeistern kann !
Wie friedsam treuer Sitten,
Getrost in That und Werk,
Liegt nicht in Deutschlands Mitten
Mein liebes Nürenberg !
Doch eines Abends spat,
Ein Unglück zu verhüten
Bei jugendheissen Gemüthen,
Ein Mann weiss sich nicht Rath ;
Ein Schuster in seinem Laden
Zieht an des Wahnes Faden :
Wie bald auf Gassen und Strassen
Fängt der da an zu rasen ;
Mann, Weib, Gesell' und Kind,
Fällt sich an wie toll und blind ;
Und will's der Wahn gesegnen,
Nun muss es Prügel regnen,
Mit Hieben, Stöss' und Dreschen
Den Wuthesbrand zu löschen.
Gott weiss, wie das geschah?
Ein Kobold half wohl da !
Ein Glühwurm fand sein Weichen nicht ;
Der hat den Schaden angericht'.

The elder's charm — Midsummer eve:
But now has dawned Midsummer day.
Let's see, then, what Hans Sachs can weave
To turn the madness his own way,
    To serve for noble works;
    For if still-here it lurks
    In Nuremberg the same,
    We'll use it to such aim
As seldom by the mob's projected,
And never without trick effected.

(*Walter enters from the chamber. He pauses a moment at the door looking at Sachs. The latter turns and allows his book to slip to the ground.*)

Sachs.

Good-day, Sir Walter! Late is my guest.
You sat up long; you've had some rest?

Walter
          (very quietly).

A little, but that rest was sound.

Sachs.

So, then, your courage you have found?

Walter.

I had a wondrous lovely dream.

Sachs.

That augurs well! Relate it, pray.

Walter.

In words I scarce dare touch its theme,
For fear it should all fade away.

Sachs.

My friend, that is the poet's art,
His dreams to cherish and impart.
Trust me, the best ideas of men
In dreams are opened to their ken:
All book-craft and all poetry
Are naught but dreams made verity.
But did your dream at all advise
How you might win the Master-prize?
But let that go;
And hark to my counsel short and strong:
Bend your mind to a Master-Song.

Walter.

A Master-Song and one that's fine:
How shall I make the two combine?

Sachs.

My friend, in youth's delightful days,
    When first in the direction
    Of blissful, true affection
The heart some power turns and sways,

Der Flieder war's: — Johannis-Nacht.—
Nun aber kam Johannis-Tag: —
Jetzt schau'n wir, wie Hans Sachs es macht,
Dass er den Wahn fein lenken mag,
Ein edles Werk zu thun;
Denn lässt er uns nicht ruh'n,
Selbst hier in Nürenberg,
So sei's um solche Werk',
Die sollten vor gemeinen Dingen,
Und nie ohn' ein'gen Wahn gelingen.—

Walther tritt unter der Kammerthüre ein. Er bleibt einen Augenblick dort stehen und blickt auf Sachs. Dieser wendet sich und lässt den Folianten auf den Boden gleiten.

Sachs.

Grüss Gott, mein Junker! Ruhtet ihr noch?
Ihr wachtet lang': nun schlieft ihr doch?

Walther
          (sehr ruhig).

Ein wenig, aber fest und gut.

Sachs.

So ist euch nun wohl bass zu Muth?

Walther.

Ich hatt' einen wunderschönen Traum.

Sachs.

Das deutet gut's! Erzählt mir den.

Walther.

Ihn selbst zu denken wag' ich kaum;
Ich fürcht' ihn mir vergeh'n zu seh'n.

Sachs.

Mein Freund, das grad' ist Dichter's Werk,
Dass er sein Träumen deut' und merk'.
Glaubt mir, des Me schen wahrster Wahn
Wird ihm im Traume aufgethan:
All' Dichtkunst und Poeterei
Ist nichts als Wahrtraum-Deuterei.
Was gilt's, es gab der Traum eu:h ein,
Wie heut' ihr sollet Sieger sein?
O, lasst dem Ruh';
Und folgt meinem Rathe, kurz und gut,
Fasst zu einem Meisterliede Muth.

Walther.

Ein schönes Lied, ein Meisterlied:
Wie fass' ich da den Unterschied?

Sachs.

Mein Freund! in holder Jugendzeit,
    Wenn uns von mächtigen Trieben
    Zum sel'gen ersten Lieben
Die Brust sich schwellet hoch und weit,

All can, or else 't were pity,
Compose a loving ditty:
For Spring cries out in ye.
But Summer, Autumn, Winter days
Bring care and sorrow often,
With wedded bliss to soften.
Children and business — frets and frays,
One who, 'spite care and duty,
Yet sings a song of beauty,
A Master he must be.

Walter.

I love a maiden and I pine
In wedlock true to make her mine.

Sachs.

Your dream alone let occupy you;
With all the rest Hans Sachs will ply you.

Walter
(places himself near Sachs, and after a moment's thought
begins in a very low voice).

" Morning was gleaming with roseate light,
The air was filled
With scent distilled,
Where, beauty beaming
Past all dreaming,
A garden did invite
My raptured sight."
(He pauses awhile.)

Sachs.

That was a stanza: now then, take heed
That one just similar may succeed.

Walter.

Why similar?

Sachs.

That folks may know
That coupled you intend to go.

Walter
(continuing).

" Over the glorious garden, behold!
With leafy crown
A tree looked down,
Majestic bending,
And extending
Its weight of fruit untold,
Like burnished gold."
(He pauses.)

Sachs.

You close not in the starting key:
The Masters hate this thing:
Hans Sachs, though, can with you agree;
It must be so in the Spring.
Now to an Aftersong proceed.

Ein schönes Lied zu singen
Mocht' vielen da gelingen;
Der Lenz, der sang für sie.
Kam Sommer, Herbst und Winterszeit,
Viel Noth und Sorg' im Leben,
Manch ehlich Glück daneben,
Kindtauf', Geschäfte, Zwist und Streit;
Denen 's dann noch will gelingen,
Ein schönes Lied zu singen,
Seht, Meister nennt man die.

Walther.

Ich lieb' ein Weib und will es frei'n
Mein dauernd Ehgemahl zu sein.

Sachs.

Gedenkt des schönen Traum's am Morgen;
Für's Andre lasst Hans Sachs nur sorgen!

Walther
(setzt sich zu Sachs, und beginnt, nach kurzer Sammlung,
sehr leise).

„ Morgenlich leuchtet in rosigem Schein,
Von Blüth' und Duft
Geschwellt die Luft,
Voll aller Wonnen
Nie ersonnen,
Ein Garten lud mich ein
Gast ihm zu sein."
(Er hält etwas an.)

Sachs.

Das war ein Stollen: nun achtet wohl,
Dass ein ganz gleicher ihm folgen soll.

Walther.

Warum ganz gleich?

Sachs.

Damit man seh'
Ihr wähltet euch gleich ein Weib zur Eh'.

Walther
(fährt fort).

„ Wonnig entragend dem seligen Raum
Bot gold'ner Frucht
Heilsaft'ge Wucht
Mit holdem Prangen
Dem Verlangen
An duft'ger Zweige Saum
Herrlich ein Baum."
(Er hält inne.)

Sachs.

Ihr scholosset nicht im gleichen Ton:
Das macht den Meistern Pein;
Doch nimmt Hans Sachs die Lehr' davon,
Im Lenz wohl müss' es so sein. —
Nun stellt mir einen Abgesang.

Walter.

What is that for?

Sachs.

> If here indeed
> A pair you 've coupled truly
> The offspring shows us duly.

Walter

(in continuation).

> " Let me confide
> What lovely miracle ensued:
> A maiden stood before my face,
> So sweet and fair I ne'er had viewed;
> Like to a bride
> She took me to her embrace;
> With bright eyes glowing,
> Her hand was showing,
> What stirred my longing profound;
> The wond'rous fruit that crowned
> The tree of life."

Sachs

(concealing his emotion).

> That is an Aftersong, I allow!
> See, the whole verse is perfect now!
> But in the melody
> You were a little free;
> I do not say that that displeases me;
> To catch it right though 's perplexing,
> A thing to our Masters vexing.
> A second verse will you please indite,
> To set the first in a clearer light?
> I cannot yet tell — your art's so supreme —
> How much was poetry, how much dream.

Walter

(as before).

> "There on the height
> A babbling stream the silence stirr'd;
> Its murm'ring tones now louder swelled,
> So sweet and strong I never heard;
> Sparkling and bright
> Distinctly the stars I beheld:
> In twinkling dances
> Among the branches
> A golden host did collect:
> Not fruit, but stars bedeck'd
> The tree of Fame." —

Sachs

(deeply moved, softly).

> Friend, your dream was well conceived;
> The second verse you have achieved.
> Now might you fashion a third verse meetly,
> To show the vision's meaning completely.

Walther.

Was soll nun der?

Sachs.

> Ob euch gelang
> Ein rechtes Paar zu finden,
> Das zeigt sich jetzt an den Kinden.

Walther

(fortfahrend).

> „Sei euch vertraut
> Welch' hehres Wunder mir gescheh'n:
> An meiner Seite stand ein Weib,
> So schön und hold ich nie geseh'n;
> Gleich einer Braut
> Umfasste sie sanft meinen Leib,
> Mit Augen winkend,
> Die Hand wies blinkend,
> Was ich verlangend begehrt,
> Die Frucht so hold und werth
> Vom Lebensbaum."

Sachs

(seine Rührung verbergend).

> Das nenn' ich mir einen Abgesang:
> Seht, wie der ganze Bar gelang!
> Nur mit der Melodei
> Seid ihr ein wenig frei;
> Doch sag' ich nicht, dass es ein Fehler sei;
> Nur ist's nicht leicht zu behalten,
> Und das ärgert unsre Alten! —
> Jetzt richtet mir noch einen zweiten Bar,
> Damit man merk', welch' der erste war.
> Auch weiss ich noch nicht, so gut ihr's gereimt,
> Was ihr gedichtet, was ihr geträumt.

Walther

(wie vorher).

> „Lieblich ein Quell
> Auf stiller Höhe dort mir rauscht;
> Jetzt schwellt er an sein hold Getön'
> So süss und stark ich's nie erlauscht:
> Leuchtend und hell
> Wie strahlten die Sterne da schön;
> Zu Tanz und Reigen
> In Laub und Zweigen
> Der gold'nen sammeln sich mehr
> Statt Frucht ein Sternenheer
> Im Lorbeerbaum."

Sachs

(sehr gerührt, sanft).

> Freund! eu'r Traumbild wies euch wahr
> Gelungen ist auch der zweite Bar.
> Wollet ihr noch einen dritten dichten,
> Des Traumes Deutung würd' er berichten.

Walter.

How can I now?   Enough of rhyme !

Sachs.

(rising).

Then we will rhyme some fitter time ! —
Lose not the tune, though, I entreat it ;
'T is fit and fair for poetry :
You shall before the world repeat it.
Hold fast the dream you 've told to me.

Walter.

What 's your intent?

Sachs.

Your servant true,
Bearing your packs, has sought for you.
The garments in the which I guessed
You meant at home to have been married
Unto my house in doubt he carried.
Some bird, sure must have shewn the nest
    Wherein his master lay.
Then follow to the chamber here !
    In costume rich and gay
'T is fitting that we both appear,
When striving for a victory.
So come, if you agree with me.

(He opens the door for Walter and goes in with him.)

Beckmesser

(peeps into the shop; finding it empty he comes in. He is
richly dressed, but in a very deplorable state. He limps,
rubs and stretches himself; then contorts himself; he tries
to sit down on a stool, but jumps quickly up and again
rubs his bruised limbs. In despair he wanders up and
down. Then pausing, he looks through the window at the
house opposite; makes gestures of wrath; strikes his hand
on his forehead. At last his eyes fall on the paper which
Sachs has written and left on the workbench; he takes it
up inquisitively, runs his eyes over it in great agitation,
and finally bursts out wrathfully) :

A Trial-song ! by Sachs? — is 't so?
Ha ! — Now then ev'rything I know !

(Hearing the chamber door open he starts and conceals the
paper hurriedly in his pocket.)

Sachs

(in holiday dress, enters and stops short).

You, sir? So early? Why this visit?
No fault of the shoes I sent you, is it?
Let 's feel ! They fit you well, I 'm sure !

Beckmesser.

Confound you !   So thin ne'er were shoes before :
Through them I feel the smallest stone.

Sachs.

My Marker's motto there is shown :
My Marker's hammer beat it so flat.

Walther.

Wie fänd ich die?   Genug der Wort' !

Sachs.

(aufstehend).

Dann Wort und That am rechten Ort ! —
D'rum bitt' ich, merkt mir gut die Weise ;
Gar lieblich d'rin sich's dichten lässt :
Und singt ihr sie in weit'rem Kreise,
Dann haltet mir auch das Traumbild fest.

Walther.

Was habt ihr vor?

Sachs.

Eu'r treuer Knecht
Fand sich mit Sack' und Tasch' zurecht ;
Die Kleider, d'rin am Hochzeitsfest
Daheim bei euch ihr wolltet prangen,
Die lies er her zu mir gelangen ; —
Ein Täubchen zeight' ihm wohl das Nest,
    Darin sein Junker träumt' :
D'rum folgt mir jetzt in's Kämmerlein !
    Mit Kleiden, wohlgesäumt,
Sollen Beide wir gezieret sein,
Wann's Stattliches zu wagen gilt : —
D'rum kommt, seid ihr gleich mir gewillt !

(Er öffnet Walther die Thür, und geht mit ihm hinein.)

Beckmesser.

(lugt zum Laden herein; da er die Werkstatt leer findet,
tritt er näher. Er ist reich aufgeputzt, aber in sehr leiden-
dem Zustande. Er hinkt, streicht und reckt sich; zuckt
wieder zusammen; er sucht einen Schemel, setzt sich;
springt aber sogleich wieder auf, und streichelt sich die
Glieder von Neuem. Verzweiflungsvoll sinnend geht er
dann umher. Dann bleibt er stehen, lugt durch das Fenster
nach dem Hause hinüber; macht Gebärden der Wuth;
schlägt sich wieder vor den Kopf. — Endlich fällt sein Blick
auf das von Sachs zuvor beschriebene Papier auf dem Werk-
tische : er nimmt es neugierig auf, überfliegt es mit immer
grösserer Aufregung, und bricht endlich wüthend aus).

Ein Werbelied ! von Sachs? — ist's wahr?
Ah ! — Nun wird mir Alles klar !

(Da er die Kammerthüre gehen hört, fährt er zusammen, und
versteckt das Blatteilig in seiner Tasche.)

Sachs

(im Festgewande, tritt ein, und hält an).

Sieh da !   Herr Schreiber?   Auch am Morgen?
Euch machen die Schuh' doch nicht mehr Sorgen?
Lasst sehen !   Mich dünkt sie sitzen gut?

Beckmesser.

Den Teufel !   So dünn war ich noch nie beschuht ·
Fühl' durch die Sohle den feinsten Kies !

Sachs.

Mein Merkersprüchlein wirkte dies :
Trieb sie mit Merkerzeichen so weich.

Beckmesser.

A merry jest! Enough of that!
Friend Sachs, I know what you are at!
    Have you forgotten quite
    What happened yesternight?
Did you not raise all that uproar, pray,
Merely to get me out of your way?

Sachs.

'T was Folly-evening: be not affrighted;
And your wedding made the people excited.
    The madder that evening's glee,
    The more blest the marriage will be.

Beckmesser
           (bursting out into a rage).

    Oh! cobbler full of cunning
    With vulgar tricks o'er-running!
    You always were my foe:
    You base designs I'll show.
    You hoary-headed reprobate!
    Attempting to appropriate
    The maiden who alone
    Is destined for my own!
    Allured by Pogner's capital
    Hans Sachs would like to snap it all;
    So, when the Guild discussed,
    He caviled and he fussed.
    But you see I got away,
    And your ill-turn I'll pay.
    Attend the singing trial,
    And see if you outvie all!
        If I'm attacked
        And badly thwacked,
I'll soon expose your wicked act!

Sachs.

Good friend, your anger makes you mad!
Think all you will of me that's bad,
But prithee calm this jealous ire;
For courtship I have no desire.

Beckmesser.

Pack of lies! I know you're double!

Sachs.

Why, Master Town-clerk, what's your trouble?
My intended plans concern not you;
But, sooth, you're deceived if you think I'd woo.

Beckmesser.

You mean to sing?

Sachs.
              Not in competing.

Beckmesser.

No wooing song?

Beckmesser

Schon gut der Witz'! Und genug der Streich'!
Glaubt mir, Freund Sachs, jetzt kenn' ich euch.
    Der spass von dieser Nacht,
    Der wird euch noch gedacht;
Dass ich euch nur nicht im Wege sei,
Schuft ihr gar Aufruhr und Meuterei!

Sachs.

's war Polterabend, lasst euch bedeuten:
Eure Hochzeit spuckte unter den Leuten;
    Je toller es da hergeh',
    Je besser bekommt's der Eh'.

Beckmesser
           (ausbrechend).

    O Schuster voll von Ränken
    Und pöbelhaften Schwänken,
    Du warst mein Feind von je:
    Nun hör' ob hell ich seh'.
    Die ich mir auserkoren,
    Die ganz für mich geboren,
    Zu aller Wittwer Schmach,
    Der Jungfer stellst du nach.
    Dass sich Herr Sachs erwerbe
    Des Goldschmied's reiches Erbe,
    Im Meister-Rath zur Hand
    Auf Klauseln er bestand,
    Doch kam ich noch so davon,
    Dass ich die That euch lohn'!
    Zieht heut' nur aus zum Singen,
    Merkt auf, wie's mag gelingen;
        Bin ich gezwackt
        Auch und zerhackt,
Euch bring' ich doch sicher aus dem Takt!

Sachs.

Gut' Freund, ihr seid in argem Wahn!
Glaubt was ihr wollt, dass ich's gethan,
Gebt eure Eifersucht nur hin;
Zu werben kommt mir nicht in Sinn.

Beckmesser.

Lug und Trug! Ich weiss es besser.

Sachs.

Was fällt euch nur ein, Meister Beckmesser?
Was ich sonst im Sinn, geht euch nichts an:
Doch glaubt, ob der Werbung, seid ihr im Wahn.

Beckmesser.

Ihr säng't heut' nicht?

Sachs.
              Nicht zur Wette.

Beckmesser.

Kein Werblied?

Sachs.

Dismiss the fear!

Beckmesser.

But I've a proof there's no defeating.

Sachs

(looking on the workbench).

Did you take the poem? I left it here.

Beckmesser

(producing the paper).

Is this not your hand?

Sachs.

Well, and what then?

Beckmesser.

The writing is fresh!

Sachs.

Still wet from the pen?

Beckmesser.

Perhaps, then, 't is a biblical song?

Sachs.

To call it so indeed were wrong.

Beckmesser.

Well, then?

Sachs.

What more?

Beckmesser.

You ask?

Sachs.

For sure!

Beckmesser.

Why, that, in all sincerity,
A most consummate rogue you must be!

Sachs.

May be! but I was never known
To pocket papers not my own;
But that you should not be called a thief,
You're welcome to it — I give you the leaf.

Beckmesser

(springing up in joyous surprise).

You do! What, a song! A song by Sachs!

(He peers sideways at the paper: suddenly he frowns.)

And yet! — If this were some villainy! —
    But yesterday you were my foe:
How, after your behavior to me,
    Such friendship can you show? —

Sachs.

Gewisslich, nein

Beckmesser.

Wenn ich aber droo ein Zeugniss hätte?

Sachs.

(blickt auf den Werktisch).

Das Gedicht? Hier liess ich's : — stecktet ihr's ein?

Beckmesser

(zieht das Blatt hervor).

Ist das eure Hand?

Sachs.

Ja, — war es das?

Beckmesser.

Ganz frisch noch die Schrift?

Sachs.

Und die Dinte noch nass i

Beckmesser.

's wär wohl gar ein biblisches Lied?

Sachs.

Der fehlte wohl, wer darauf rieth.

Beckmesser.

Nun denn?

Sachs.

Wie doch?

Beckmesser.

Ihr fragt?

Sachs.

Was noch?

Beckmesser.

Dass ihr mit aller Biederkeit
Der ärgste aller Spitzbuben seid!

Sachs.

Mag sein! Doch hab' ich noch nie entwandt,
Was ich auf fremden Tischen fand:
Und dass man von euch auch nicht übels denkt,
Behaltet das Blatt, es sei euch geschenkt.

Beckmesser

(in freudigem Schreck aufspringend).

Herr Gott! . . Ein Gedicht! . . Ein Gedicht von
    Sachs? . .

(Er blickt seitwärts in das Blatt: plötzlich runzelt sich seine
Stirn.)

Und doch! Wenn's nur eine Falle wär'! —
    Noch gestern war't ihr mein Feind
Wie käm's, dass nach so grosser Beschwer
    Ihr's freundlich heut' mit mir meint?

Sachs.

I sat up late to make your shoes:
It is not thus our foes we use.

Beckmesser.

Aye, aye ! that 's true !— But one thing swear:
That when you hear this, no matter where !
To nobody shall be disclosed
The fact that 't was by you composed.

Sachs.

I swear it and I guarantee
That none shall know the song 's by me.

Beckmesser
(very joyous).

What more remains?   I 'm joyful-hearted !
Beckmesser's troubles have departed !
(He rubs his hands with elation.)
Farewell, I 'm away !
Some other day,
When in this latitude,
I 'll pay my gratitude
For your kind attitude ;
Buy all your works, you know ;
You shall as Marker show ; —
Chalk you must mark with, though,
Not with the hammer's blow !
Marker !   Marker !   Marker Hans Sachs !
May he and Nuremberg bloom and wax !
(As if intoxicated he limps, stumbling and blundering,
away.)

Sachs.

I ne'er met with so evil a man :
He 'll come to grief one of these days.
Their reason most men squander who can,
Yet keep some little relays :
But some weak moments all discover ;
Then they are fools and we talk them over. —
That Master Beckmesser wasn't square,
Finely will further my affair. —
(Through his window he sees Eva approaching.)
Ha, Eva !   Here she is, I declare !
(Eva, richly tricked out and in a gleaming white dress,
enters the shop.)

Sachs.

My child, good morning !   Ah ! how pretty
And smart you are to-day !
Both old and young — why, all the city
You 'll win in such array.

Eva.

Master, surely now you flatter !
And if my dress is all right,
Will no one notice what 's the matter?
My shoe is much too tight.

Sachs.

Ich machte euch Schuh' in später Nacht :
Hat man so je einen Feind bedacht?

Beckmesser.

Ja ja ! recht gut !— doch Eines schwört :
Wo und wie ihr das Lied auch hört,
Dass nie ihr euch beikommen lass't,
Zu sagen, es sei von Euch verfasst.

Sachs.

Das schwör ich und gelob' euch hier,
Nie mich zu rühmen, das Lied sei von mir.

Beckmesser
(sehr glücklich).

Was will ich mehr, ich bin geborgen !
Jetzt hat sich Beckmesser nicht mehr zu sorgen !
(Er reibt sich froh die Hände.)
Ade-! ich muss fort !
An and'rem Ort
Dank' ich euch inniglich,
Weil ihr so minniglich ;
Für euch nun stimme ich,
Kauf' eure Werke gleich,
Mache zum Merker euch :
Doch fein mit Kreide weich,
Nicht mit dem Hammerstreich !
Merker !   Merker !   Merker Hans Sachs !
Dass Nürnberg schusterlich blüh' und wachs' !
(Er hinkt, poltert und taumelt wie besessen fort.)

Sachs.

So ganz boshaft doch keinen ich fand,
Er hält's auf die Länge nicht aus :
Vergeudet mancher oft viel Verstand,
Doch hält er auch damit Haus :
Die schwache Stunde kommt für Jeden ;
Da wird er dumm und lässt mit sich reden. —
Dass hier Herr Beckmesser ward zum Dieb,
Ist mir für meinen Plan sehr lieb.
(Er sieht durch das Fenster Eva kommen.)
Sieh, Evchen !   Dacht' ich doch, wo sie blieb' !
(Eva, reich geschmückt und in glänzender weisser Kleidung
tritt zum Laden herein.)

Sachs.

Grüss' Gott, mein Evchen !   Ei, wie herrlich,
Wie stolz du's heute meinst !
Du machst wohl Jung und Alt begehrlich,
Wenn du so schön erscheinst.

Eva.

Meister ! 's ist nicht so gefährlich :
Und ist's dem Schneider geglückt,
Wer sieht dann an wo's mir beschwerlich,
Wo still der Schuh mich drückt?

Sachs.

The naughty shoe!   But 't was your haste;
You would not try it on, you see.

Eva.

Not so; too great a trust I placed:
The Master's disappointed me.

Sachs.

I'm really griev'd!   Come here, my pet,
And I will help you even yet.

Eva.

If I would stand, it will away;
Would I begone, it makes me stay.

Sachs.

Upon the stool here place your foot.
A shocking fault!   I'll look into 't.

    (She puts her foot upon a stool by the workbench.)

What is amiss?

Eva.

        Too wide, you see.

Sachs.

Child, that is purely vanity:
The shoe is tight.

Eva.

        I told you so,
And that is why it hurts my toe.

Sachs.

Here — left?

Eva.

        No, right.

Sachs.

        What!   On the sole?

Eva.

Here, at the ankle.

Sachs.

        Well!   That's droll!

Eva.

Nay, Master! do you know better than I
Where the shoe pinches?

Sachs.

        I wonder why,
If it's too wide, it pinches you so.

Walter, in glittering knightly apparel, appears at the chamber door, and stands there spellbound at the sight of Eva. She utters a slight cry, but remains in her position with one foot on the stool.   Sachs is kneeling before her with his back towards the door.

Sachs.

Der böse Schuh!   's war deine Laun',
Dass du ihn gestern nicht probirt.

Eva.

Merk' wohl, ich hatt' zu viel Vertrau'n:
Im Meister hab' ich mich geirrt.

Sachs.

Ei, 's thut mir leid!   Zeig' her, mein Kind,
Dass ich dir helfe, gleich geschwind.

Eva.

Sobald ich stehe, will es geh'n:
Doch will ich geh'n, zwingt's mich zu steh'n.

Sachs.

Heir auf den Schemel streck' den Fuss:
Der üblen Noth ich wehren muss.

    (Sie streckt den Fuss auf den Schemel beim Werktisch.)

Was ist's mit dem?

Eva.

        Ihr sekt, zu weit!

Sachs.

Kind, dat ist pure Eitelkeit:
Der Schuh ist knapp.

Eva.

        Das sag' ich ja:
Drum drückt er mir die Zehen da.

Sachs.

Hier links?

Eva.

        Nein, rechts.

Sachs.

        Wohl mehr am Spann?

Eva.

Mehr hier am Hacken.

Sachs.

        Kommt der auch dran?

Eva.

Ach Meister!   Wüsstet ihr besser als ich,
Wo der Schuh mich drückt?

Sachs.

        Ei, 's wundert mich
Dass er zu weit, und doch drückt überall?

Walther, in glänzender Rittertracht, tritt unter die Thüre der Kammer, und bleibt beim Anblick Eva's wie festgebannt stehen.   Eva stösst einen leisen Schrei aus und bleibt ebenfalls unverwandt in ihrer Stellung, mit dem Fusse au dem Schemel.   Sachs, der vor ihr sich gebückt hat, ist mit dem Rücken der Thüre zugekehrt.

Aha! 't is here! Now the reason I know!
Child, you are right: 't is in the *sole!*
One moment, and I 'll make it whole.
Stand so awhile, I 'll fasten your shoe
On the last a moment, then it will do.

(He has gently drawn off her shoe; while she remains in the same position he pretends to busy himself with it, and to be oblivious of all else.)

Sachs

(as he works).

Cobbling always! That is my fate;
I keep it up both early and late.
Hark ye, child! I 've given it much thought,
How should my work to an end be brought.
The best way 's to join the contest for you;
I should win some fame as a poet too.
Come now, reply! You do not heed!
'T was you put that in my head indeed!
All right! You say, "Stick to your shoes!"
Will some one give us a song to amuse?
I heard to-day a lovely one;
Let 's see if the third verse can be done!

Walter

(still in the same position opposite Eva).

" Lingered the stars in their dance of delight?
　　They rested there
　　Upon her hair,
　　That wondrous maiden
　　So beauty-laden.
And formed a circlet bright
　　All star bedight,
Wonder on wonder now waked my surprise;
　　The light of day
　　Had twofold ray;
　　For two transcendent
　　Suns resplendent
Within her heavenly eyes
　　I saw arise.
　　Image so rare,
Which boldly I approached and viewed!
By all this light the crown above
At once was faded and renewed.
　　Tender and fair
She wove it round the head of her love.
　　Thus grace-directed,
　　To fame elected,
She poured the joys of the blest
Into the poet's breast,
　　In Love's sweet dream."

Sachs

(busily at work, brings back the shoe during the last verse of Walter's song and fits it on Eva's foot again).

Hark, child! that is a Master-song;
You hear such music where I dwell now.
So try if still my shoe is wrong.

Aha! hier sitzt's! Nun begreif' ich den Fall!
Kind, du hast recht: 's stack in der Nath: —
Nun warte, dem Uebel schaff' ich Rath.
Bleib' nur so steh'n; ich nehm' dir den Schuh
Eine Weil' auf den Leisten: dann lässt er dir Ruh'.

(Er hat ihr sanft den Schuh vom Fusse gezogen; während sie in ihrer Stellung verbleibt, macht er sich mit dem Schuh zu schaffen, und thut, als beachte er nichts andres.)

Sachs

(bei der Arbeit).

Immer Schustern! das ist nun mein Loos;
Des Nachts, des Tags — komm' nicht davon los! —
Kind, hör' zu! Ich hab's überdacht,
Was meinem Schustern ein Ende macht:
Am Besten, ich werbe doch noch um dich;
Da gewänn' ich doch 'was als Poet für mich! —
Du hörst nicht drauf? — So sprich doch jetzt!
Hast mir's ja selbst in den Kopf gesetzt?
Schon gut! — ich merk'! — Mach deinen Schuh! ...
Säng' mir nur wenigstens Einer dazu!
Hörte heut' gar ein schönes Lied: —
Wem dazu ein dritter Vers gerieth'!

Walther.

(immer Eva gegenüber in der vorigen Stellung).

„Weilten die Sterne im lieblichen Tanz?
　　So licht und klar
　　Im Lockenhaar,
　　Vor allen Frauen
　　Hehr zu schauen,
　　Lag ihr mit zartem Glanz
　　Ein Sternenkranz. —
Wunder ob Wunder nun bieten sich dar:
　　Zwiefachen Tag
　　Ich grüssen mag;
　　Denn Gleich zwei'n Sonnen
　　Reinster Wonnen,
　　Der hehrsten Augen Paar
　　Nahm ich nun wahr. —
　　Huldreichstes Bild,
　　Dem ich zu nahen mich erkühnt:
Den Kranz, vor zweier Sonnen Strahl
Zugleich verblichen und ergrünt,
　　Minnig und mild,
　　Sie flocht ihn um's Haupt dem Gemahl
　　Dort Huld-geboren,
　　Nun Rhum-erkoren,
　　Giesst paradiesche Lust
　　Sie in des Dichters Brust —
　　Im Liebstraum." —

Sachs

(hat, immer mit seiner Arbeit beschäftigt, den Schuh zurück-gebracht, und ist jetzt während der Schlussverse von Walther's Gesang daruber her, ihn Eva wieder anzuziehen).

Lausch', Kind! das ist ein Meisterlied:
Derlei hörst du jetzt bei mir singen.
Nun schau', ob dabei mein Schuh gerieth?

Was I not right?
And fits it well now?
Let 's see ! Stand down ! Is it still tight?

(Eva, who has stood still as if enchanted, gazing and listening, bursts into a sudden fit of weeping and sinks on Sachs's breast, sobbing and clinging to him. — Walter advances toward them and wrings Sachs's hand in silent ecstasy. — Sachs at last composes himself, tears himself gloomily away and causes Eva to rest unconsciously on Walter's shoulder.)

Eva

(stops Sachs and draws him to her again).

O Sachs ! best friend and dearest ! Say
How can I e'er my debt repay?
   Bereft of thy great kindness
   How helpless should I be !
   Still wrapped in childish blindness
   Had it not been for thee.
      Through thee life's treasure
      I control,
      Through thee I measure
      First my soul.
      Through thee I wake ;
      My feelings take
A higher, nobler tone :
I bloom through thee alone ! —
Yes, dearest Master, scold you may !

Sachs.

   My child :
Sir Tristan I have read of —
Isolde's story dark :
Hans Sachs had prudent dread of
The fate of poor king Mark. —
'T was time the right man did appear,
Or I should have been caught, I fear ! —
Aha ! There 's Magdalena 's found us out.
Come in ! — Ho, David ! — What 's he about?

(Magdalena in holiday attire enters from the street and David at the same time comes out of the chamber, also gayly dressed and very splendid with ribbons and flowers.)

The witnesses wait, the sponsors are found ;
So now for a christening gather around !

   (All look at him with surprise.)

   A child here was created ;
   Let its name by you be stated.
Such is the Masters' constant use,
When they a Master-song produce :
They give it a fitly chosen name
That men may know it by the same.
   So let me tell all you here
   What 't is we have to do here !
A Master-song has been completed,
By young Sir Walter made and repeated ;
The newborn poem's father, delighted,
For sponsors has Eva and me invited :

Mein' endlich doch.
Es thät' mir gelingen?
Versuch's ! tritt auf ! — Sag', drückt er dich noch !

(Eva, die wie bezaubert bewegungslos gestanden, gesehen und gehört hat, bricht jetzt in heftiges Weinen aus, sinkt Sachs an die Brust und drückt ihn schluchzend an sich. — Walther ist zu ihnen getreten, und druckt Sachs begeistert die Hand. — Sachs thut sich endlich Gewalt an, reisst sich wie unmuthig los, und lässt dadurch Eva unwillkürlich an Walther's Schulter sich anlehnen.)

Eva

(hält Sachs, und zieht ihn von Neuem zu sich).

O Sachs ! Mein Freund ! Du theurer Mann !
Wie ich dir Edlem lohnen kann !
   Was ohne deine Liebe,
   Was wär' ich ohne dich,
   Ob je auch Kind ich bliebe
   Erwecktest du nicht mich?
      Durch dich gewann ich
      Was man preist.
         Durch dich ersann ich
         Was ein Geist !
         Durch dich erwacht,
         Durch dich nur dacht'
   Ich edel, frei und kühn :
   Du liessest mich erblüh'n ! —
O lieber Meister ! schilt mich nur !

Sachs.

   Mein Kind :
   Von Tristan und Isolde
   Kenn' ich ein traurig Stück :
   Hans Sachs war klug, und wollte
   Nichts von Herrn Marke's Gluck. —
's war Zeit, dass ich den Rechten erkannt :
Wär' sonst am End' doch hineingerannt !
Aha ! da streicht schon die Lene um's Haus,
Nur herein ! — He, David ! Kommst nicht heraus?

(Magdalene, in festlichem Staate, tritt durch die Ladenthür herein; aus der Kammer kommt zugleich David, ebenfalls im Festkleid, mit Blumen und Bändern sehr reich und zierlich ausgeputzt.)

Die Zeugen sind da, Gevatter, zur Hand ;
Jetzt schnell zur Taufe ; nehmt euren Stand !

   (Alle blicken ihn verwundert an.)

   Ein Kind ward hier geboren ;
   Jetzt sei ihm ein Nam' erkoren !
So ist's nach Meister-Weis' und Art,
Wenn eine Meisterweise geschaffen ward :
Dass die einen guten Namen trag',
Dran Jeder sie erkennen mag. —
   Vernehmt, respectable Gesellschaft,
   Was euch hierher zur Stell' schafft !
Eine Meisterweise ist gelungen,
Von Junker Walther gedichtet und gesungen ;
Der jungen Weise lebender Vater
Lud mich und die Pognerin zu Gevatter ;

As to the song we have been list'ning
We now come hither to its christ'ning.
To see that we act with solemn fitness
Shall David and Lena be called to witness:
But as no Prentice a witness can be,
And as he's repeated his task to me,
A Journeyman I will make him here.
Kneel, David, and take this box on the ear.

(David kneels and Sachs gives h.m a smart box on the ear.)

Arise, my man; remember that blow;
I will mark this baptism for you, you know.
Lacks aught beside, what blame indeed?
Who knows if private baptism we need?
That the melody lack not anything vital
I now proceed to give it its title.
" The glorious morning-dream's true story." —
So be it named, to the Master's glory.
And may it increase in size and strength. —
I bid the young god-mother speak at length.

Eva.

Dazzling as the dawn
That smiles upon my glee,
Rapture-laden morn
To bliss awakens me.
Dream of palmy beauty,
Brilliant morning-glow!
Hard but sweet the duty
Thy intent to know.
That divine and tender strain
With its tones of gladness
Has revealed my heart's sweet pain
And subdued its sadness.
It is but a morning-dream?
Scarcely real doth it seem.
What the ditty,
Soft and pretty,
Told to me,
A quiet theme,
Loud and free.
In the Masters' conclave wise
Shall achieve the highest prize.

Walter.

'T was thy love — the highest gain —
Allured me by its gladness,
To reveal my heart's sweet pain
And subdue its sadness,
Is it still my morning-dream?
Scarcely real doth it seem.
What the ditty,
Soft and pretty,
Told to thee,
A quiet theme,
Loud and free
In the Masters' conclave wise
Shall achieve the highest prize.

Weil wir die Weise wohl vernommen,
Sind wir zur Taufe hierher gekommen.
Auch dass wir zur Handlung Zeugen haben,
Ruf' ich Jungfer Lene, und meinen Knaben:
Doch da's zum Zeugen kein Lehrbube thut,
Und heut' auch den Spruch er gesungen gut,
So mach' ich den Burschen gleich zum Gesell':
Knie' nieder, David, und nimm diese Schell'!

(David ist niedergekniet: Sachs giebt ihm eine starke
Ohrfeige.)

Steh' auf, Gesell! und denk' an den Streich:
Du merkst dir dabei die Taufe zugleich!
Fehlt sonst noch 'was, uns Keiner drum schilt:
Wer weiss ob's nicht ger eine Nothtaufe gilt.
Dass die Weise Kraft bahalte zum Leben,
Will ich uur gleich den Numen ihr geben: —
„ Die selige Morgentraumdeut-Weise "
Sei sie genannt zu des Meisters Preise.
Nun wachse sie gross, ohn' Schad' und Bruch:
Die jüngste Gevatt'rin spricht den Spruch.

Eva.

Selig, wie die Sonne
Meines Glückes lacht,
Morgen voller Wonne,
Selig mir erwacht!
Traum der höchsten Hulden,
Himmlisch Morgenglüh'n!
Deutung euch zu schulden,
Selig süss Bemüh'n'!
Einer Weise mild und hehr,
Sollt' es hold gelingen,
Meines Herzens süss Beschwer
Deutend zu bezwingen.
Ob es nur ein Morgentraum?
Selig' deut' ich mir es kaum.
Doch die Weise,
Was sie leise
Mir vertraut
Im stillen Raum,.
Hell und laut,
In der Meister volleim Kreis,
Deute sie den höchsten Preis!

Walther.

Deine Liebe, rein und hehr,
Liess es mir gelingen,
Meines Herzens süss Beschwer
Deutend zu bezwingen.
Ob es noch der Morgentraum?
Selig deut' ich mir es kaum.
Doch die Weise,
Was sie leise
Dir vertraut
Im stillen Raum,
Hell und laut,
In der Meister vollem Kreis,
Werbe sie um höchsten Preis!

Sachs.

    With the maiden I would fain
        Sing for very gladness ;
    But my heart I must restrain,
        Quell my passion's madness.
    'T was a tender evening-dream :
    Undiscovered let it beam.
        What the ditty,
        Soft and pretty,
        Told to me
        In quiet theme,
        Here I see :
    Youth and love that never dies
    Flourish through the master-prize.

David.

    Am I awake or dreaming still?
    Scarce to explain it have I skill.
    Sure 't is but a morning-dream !
    All these things unreal seem.
        Can it be, man,
        You 're a freeman?
        And that she —
        Oh, joy supreme ! —
        My spouse shall be?
    Round and round my headpiece flies
    That a Master I now rise !

Magdalena.

    Am I awake or dreaming still?
    Scarce to explain it have I skill.
    Sure 't is, but a morning-dream !
    All these things unreal seem.
        Can it be, man,
        You 're a freeman?
        And that we —
        Oh, joy supreme ! —
        Shall wedded be?
    Yes, what honor near me lies?
    Soon I shall as Madam rise !

(The orchestra goes into a broad march-like theme.—Sachs
        makes the group break up.)

Sachs.

Now let 's be off ! — Your father stays !
Quick, to the fields all go your ways !

Eva tears herself away from Sachs and Walter and leaves
      the house with Magdalena.)

So come, sir knight ! take heart of grace !
David, my man, lock up the place.

  As Sachs and Walter also go into the street, and David is
left shutting up the shop, curtains descend from each side of
the proscenium so as to conceal the stage. — When the
music has gradually swelled to the loudest pitch the curtains
are drawn up again and the scene is changed.

Sachs.

    Vor dem Kinde lieblich hehr,
        Mocht' ich gern wohl singen ;
    Doch des Herzens süss Beschwer
        Galt es zu bezwingen.
    's war ein schöner Abendtraum :
    Dran zu deuten wag ich kaum.
        Diese Weise,
        Was sie leise,
        Mir vertraut
        Im stillen Raum,
        Sagt mir laut :
    Auch der Jugend ew'ges Reis
    Grünt nur durch des Dichters Preis.

David.

    Wach' oder träum' ich schon so früh'?
    Das zu erklären macht mir Müh'.
    's ist wohl nur ein Morgentraum?
    Was ich seh', begreif' ich kaum.
        Ward zur Stelle
        Gleich Geselle?
        Lene Braut?
        Im Kirchenraum
        Wir getraut?
    's geht der Kopf mir, wie im Kreis,
    Dass ich bald gar Meister heiss' !

Magdalene.

    Wach' oder träum' ich schon so früh?
    Das zu erklären macht mir Müh' !
    's ist wohl nur ein Morgentraum?
    Was ich seh', begreif' ich kaum.
        Er, zur Stelle
        Gleich Geselle?
        Ich die Braut?
        Im Kirchenraum
        Wir getraut?
    Ja, wahrhaftig ! 's geht : wer weiss?
    Bald ich wohl Frau Meist'rin heiss' !

(Das Orchester geht sehr leise in eine marschmässige, heitere
    Weise über. — Sachs ordnet den Aufbruch an.)

Sachs.

    Jetzt All' am Fleck !   Den Vater küss' !
    Auf, nach der Wies', schnell auf die Füss'.

(Eva trehnt sich von Sachs und Walther und verlässt mit
      Magdalene die Werkstatt.)

Nun, Junker !   Kommt !   Habt frohen Muth ! —
David' Gesell' !   Schliess den Laden gut !

  Als Sachs und Walther ebenfalls auf die Strasse gehen,
und David sich über das Schliessen der Ladenthüre her-
macht, wird im Proscenium ein Vorhang von beiden Seiten
zusammengezogen, so dass er die Scene gänzlich schliesst. —
Als die Musik allmählich zu grösserer Stärke angewachsen ist,
wird der Vorhang nach der Höhe zu aufgezogen.   Die
Bühne ist verwandelt.

CHANGE OF SCENE.

The stage now represents an open meadow; in the distance at back the town of Nuremberg. The Pegnitz winds across the plain; the narrow river is practicable in the foreground. Boats gaily decorated with flags continually discharge fresh parties of Burghers of the different Guilds with their wives and families, who land on the banks. A raised stand with benches on it is erected R, already adorned with flags of those as yet arrived; as the scene opens, the standard-bearers of freshly arriving Guilds also place their banners against the Singer's stage, so that it is at last quite closed in on three sides by them. Tents with all kinds of refreshments border the sides of the open space in front.

Before the tents is much merry-making: Burghers and their families sit and group round them.— The Prentices of the Master-singers, in holiday attire, finely decked out with ribbons and flowers, and bearing slender wands, also ornamented, fulfil frolicsomely the office of heralds and stewards. They receive the new comers on the bank, arrange them in procession and conduct them to the stand, whence, after the standard-bearer has deposited his banner, the Burghers and Journeymen disperse under the tents.

Among the arriving Guilds the following are prominent.

The Shoemakers.
   (As they march past.)
 Saint Crispin !
 Honor him !
He was both wise and good,
 Did all a cobbler could.
That was a fine time for the poor !
 He made them all warm shoes ;
When none would lend him leather more,
  To steal he 'd not refuse.
  The cobbler has a conscience easy,
  No obstacles to labor sees he ;
  When from the tanner 't is sent away
   Then hey ! hey ! hey !
Leather becomes his rightful prey.

(The Town-pipers, Lute- and Toy-instrument-makers, playing on their instruments, follow. These are succeeded by)

The Tailors.
When Nuremberg besieged did stand
 And famine wrought despair,
Undone had been both folk and land
 Had not a tailor been there
 Of craft and courage rare :
Within a goatskin he did hide
And showed upon the wall outside,
 There took to gaily tripping
 And gambolling and skipping.
The foe beheld it with dismay :
" The devil fetch that town away

VERWANDLUNG.

Die Scene stellt einen freien Wiesenplan dar, im fernen Hintergrunde die Stadt Nürnberg. Die Pegnitz schlängelt sich durch den Plan : der schmale Fluss ist an den nächsten Punkten praktikabel gehalten. Buntbeflaggte Kähne setzen unablässig die noch ankommenden, festlich geschmückten Bürger der Zunfte, mit Frauen und Kindern, an das Ufer der Festwiese über. Eine erhöhte Buhne mit Bänken darauf ist rechts zur Seite aufgeschlagen ; bereits ist sie mit den Fahnen der angekommenen Zunfte ausgeschmückt ; im Verlaufe stecken die Fahnenträger der noch ankommenden Zunfte ihre Fahnen ebenfalls um die Sängerbühne auf, so dass diese schliesslich nach drei Seiten hin ganz davon eingefasst ist.— Zelte mit Getränken und Erfrischungen aller Art begrenzen im Uebrigen die Seiten des vorderen Hauptraumes.

Vor den Zelten geht es bereits lustig her : Bürger mit Frauen und Kindern sitzen und lagern daselbst.— Die Lehrbuben der Meistersinger festlich gekleidet, mit Blumen und Bändern reich und anmuthig geschmückt, üben mit schlanken Stäben, die ebenfalls mit Blumen und Bändern reich geziert sind, in lustiger Weise das Amt von Herolden und Marschällen aus. Sie empfangen die am Ufer Aussteigenden, ordnen die Züge der Zünfte, und geleiten diese nach der Singerbühne, von wo aus, nachdem der Bannerträger die Fahne aufgepflanzt, die Zunftbürger und Gesellen nach Belieben sich unter den Zelten zerstreuen.

Unter den noch anlangenden Zünften werden die folgenden besonders bemerkt.

Die Schuster.
   (Indem sie aufziehen.)
 Sankt Crispin,
 Lobet ihn !
War gar ein heilig Mann,
 Zeigt was ein Schuster kann.
Die Armen hatten gute Zeit,
 Macht' ihnen warme Schuh' ;
Und wenn ihm Keiner Leder leiht',
 So stahl er sich's dazu.
 Der Schuster hat ein weit Gewissen,
 Macht Schuhe selbst mit Hindernissen ;
 Und ist vom Gerber das Fell erst weg,
  Dann streck' ! streck' ! streck' !
Leder taugt nur am rechten Fleck.

(Die Stadtpfeifer, Lauten- und Kinderinstrumentmacher ziehen, auf ihren Instrumenten spielend, auf Ihnen folgen.)

Die Schneider. Als Nürnberg belagert war,
 Und Hungersnoth sich fand,
Wär' Stadt und Volk verdorben gar,
 War nicht ein Schneider zur Hand.
 Der viel Muth hat und Verstand :
Hat sich in ein Bockfell eingenäht,
Auf dem Stadtwall da springen geht,
 Und macht wohl seine Sprünge
 Gar lustig guter Dinge.
Der Feind, der sieht's und zieht vom Fleck :
Der Teufel hol' die Stadt sich weg,

Where goats yet merrily play, play, play.
Me-ey! me-ey! me-ey!
(Imitating the bleating of a goat.)
Who 'd think that a tailor within there lay?

The Bakers.
(Coming close behind the Tailors, so that the two songs
join together.)
Want of bread! Want of bread!
That is a hardship true, sirs!
If you were not by the baker fed
Old Death would feed on you, sirs.
Pray! pray! pray!
Baker every day,
Hunger turn away!

Prentices.
Heyday! Heyday! Maidens from Fürth!
Play up, town-piper, one merry spurt!

(A gaily painted boat, filled with young Girls in fine
peasant-costumes, arrives. The Prentices help the Girls
out and dance with them, while the town-pipers play,
towards the front.—The character of this dance consists
in the Prentices appearing only to wish to bring the Girls
to the open place; the Journeymen endeavor to capture
them and the Prentices move on as if seeking another
place, thus making the tour of the stage and continually
delaying their original purpose in fun and frolic.)

David.
(Advancing from the landing-place.)
You dance! The Masters will rate such folly.
(The boys make faces at him.)
Do n't care? Why, then, let me too be jolly!
(He seizes a young and pretty girl and mingles in the
dance with great ardor. The spectators notice him and
laugh.)

Some of the Prentices.
David! there 's Lena! There s Lena sees
you!

David.
(Alarmed hastily releases the maiden, but seeing noth-
ing, quickly regains his courage and resumes his dancing.)
Have done with your silly jokes, my boys, do !

Journeymen.
(At the landing-place.)
The Master-singers! the Master-singers!

David.
Oh, lor'!—Farewell, ye pretty clingers!
(He gives the maiden an ardent kiss and tears himself
away. The Prentices quickly discontinue their dance,
hasten to the bank and arrange themselves to receive the
Master-singers. All stand back, by command of the
Prentices.—The Master-singers arrange their procession
on the bank and then march forwards to take their places
on the stand. First Kothner, as standard-bearer, then
Pogner leading Eva by the hand; she is attended by
richly dressed Maidens among whom is Magdalena. Then
follow the other Master-singers. They are greeted with
cheers and waving of hats. When all have reached the

Hat's drin noch so lustige Meck-meck-meck!
Meck! Meck! Meck!
(Das Gemecker der Ziege nachahmend.)
Wer glaubt's, dass ein Schneider im Bocke
steck'!

Die Bäcker.
(Ziehen dicht hinter den Schneidern auf, so dass ihr
Lied in das der Schneider hineinklingt.)
Hungersnoth! Hungersnoth!
Das ist ein gräulich Leiden!
Gäb' euch der Bäcker kein täglich Brod,
Müsst' alle Welt verscheiden.
Beck! Beck! Beck!
Täglich auf dem Fleck!
Nimm uns den Hunger weg!

Lehrbuben.
Herr Je! Herr Je! Mädel von Fürth!
Stadtpfeifer spielt! dass 's lustig wird!

(' .. bunter Kahn, mit jungen Mädchen in reicher
bäuerischer Tracht, ist angekommen. Die Lehrbuben
heben die Mädchen heraus, und tanzen mit ihnen, während
die Stadtpfeifer spielen, nach dem Vordergrunde. Das
Charakteristische des Tanzes besteht darin, dass die
Lehrbuben die Mädchen scheinbar nur an den Platz
bringen wollen; sowie die Gesellen zug eifen wollen,
ziehen die Buben die Mädchen aber immer wieder zurück,
als ob sie sie anderswo unterbringen wollten, wobei sie
meistens den ganzen Kreis, wie wühlend, ausmessen, und
somit die scheinbare Absicht auszuführen, anmuthig und
lustig verzögern.)

David.
(Kommt vom Landungsplatze vor.)
Ihr tanzt? Was werden die Meister sagen?
(Die Buben drehen ihm Nasen.)
Hört nicht? — Lass' ich mir's auch beha-
gen!
(Er nimmt sich ein junges, schönes Mädchen, und
geräth im Tanze mit ihr bald in grosses Feuer. Die
Zuschauer freuen sich und lachen.)

Ein paar Lehrbuben.
David! die Lene! die Lene sieht zu!

David.
(Erschrickt, lässt das Mädchen schnell fahren, fasst sich
aber Muth, da er nichts sieht, und tanzt noch feuriger
weiter.)
Ach! lasst mich mit euren Possen in Ruh'!
Gesellen.
(Am Landungsplatz.)
Die Meistersinger! Die Meistersinger!

David.
Herr Gott!—Ade, ihr hübschen Dinger!
(Er giebt dem Mädchen einen feurigen Kuss und reisst
sich los. Die Lehrbuben unterbrechen alle schnell den
Tanz, eilen zum Ufer und reihen sich dort zum Empfang
der Meistersinger. Alles macht auf das Geheiss der
Lehrbuben Platz.—Die Meistersinger ordnen sich am
Landungsplatze und ziehen dann festlich auf, um auf
der erhöhten Bühne ihre Plätze einzunehmen. Voran
Kothner als Fahnenträger; dann Pogner, Eva an der
Hand führend; diese ist von festlich geschmückten
und reich gekleideten jungen Mädchen begleitet, denen
sich Magdalene anschliesst. Dann folgen die übrigen

platform, Eva has taken the place of honor, with her Maidens round her, and Kothner has placed his banner in the middle of the others, which it overtops; the Prentices solemnly advance in rank and file before the stand, turning to the people.)

Prentices.

Silentium! Silentium!

Make no sound, e'en the merest hum!

(Sachs rises and steps forward. At sight of him all burst out into fresh acclamations and wavings of hats and kerchiefs.)

All the People.

Ha! Sachs! 'T is Sachs!

See! Master Sachs!

Sing all! Sing all! Sing all!
(With solemn delivery.)

" Awake! draws nigh the break of day:

" I hear upon the hawthorn spray

" A bonny little nightingale;

" His voice resounds o'er hill and dale.

" The night descends the western sky

" And from the east the morn draws nigh,

" With ardor red the flush of day

" Breaks through the cloud-bank dull and grey."

Hail, Sachs! Hans Sachs!

Hail, Nuremberg's darling Sachs!

(Long silence of deep feeling. Sachs, who, as if wrapt, has stood motionless, gazing far away beyond the multitude, at last turns a genial glance on them, bows courteously and begins in a voice at first trembling with emotion but soon gaining firmness.)

Sachs.

Your hearts you ease, mine you oppress,

I feel my own unworthiness.

What I must prize all else above

Is your esteem and honest love.

Already honor I have gained,

To-day as spokesman I 'm ordained;

And in the matter of my speech,

You will be honored, all and each.

If Art so much you honor, sirs,

We ought to show you rather

That one who 's altogether hers

Esteems her even farther.

A Master, noble, rich, and wise,

Will prove you this with pleasure:

His only child, the highest prize

With all his wealth and treasure,

He offers as inducement strong

To him who in the art of song

Before the people here

As victor shall appear.

So hear my words and follow me:

To poets all this trial 's free.

Ye Masters who compete to-day,

To you before all here I say:

Bethink you what a prize this is!

Let each, if he would win it,

Meistersinger. Sie werden mit Hutschwenken und Freudenrufen begrüsst. Als Alle auf der Bühne angelangt sind, Eva, von den Mädchen umgeben, den Ehrenplatz eingenommen, und Kothner die Fahne gerade in der Mitte der übrigen Fahnen, und sie alle überragend, aufgepflanzt hat, treten die Lehrbuben, dem Volke zugewendet, feierlich vor der Bühne in Reih und Glied.

Lehrbuben. Silentium! Silentium!

Lasst all' Reden und Gesumm'!

(Sachs erhebt sich und tritt vor. Bei seinem Anblick stösst sich sofort Alles an und bricht sofort unter Hut- und Tücherschwenken in grossen Jubel aus.)

Alles Volk. Ha! Sachs! 's ist Sachs!

Seht! Meister Sachs!

Stimmt an! Stimmt an! Stimmt an!
(Mit feierlicher Haltung.)

" Wach' auf, es nahet gen den Tag,

" Ich hör' singen im grünen Hag

" Ein wonnigliche Nachtigall,

" Ihr Stimm' durchklinget Berg und Thal:

" Die Nacht neigt sich zum Occident,

" Der Tag geht auf von Orient,

" Die rothbrünstige Morgenröth'

" Her durch die trüben Wolken geht."

Heil Sachs! Hans Sachs!

Heil Nürnberg's theurem Sachs!

(Längeres Schweigen grosser Ergriffenheit. — Sachs der unbeweglich, wie geistesabwesend, über die Volksmenge hinweg geblickt hatte, richtet endlich seine Blicke vertrauter auf sie, verneigt sich freundlich, und beginnt mit ergriffener, schnell aber sich festigender Stimme.)

Sachs.

Euch wird es leicht, mir macht ihr's schwer,

Gebt ihr mir Armen zu viel Ehr':

Such' vor der Ehr' ich zu besteh'n,

Sei's, mich von euch geliebt zu seh'n!

Schon grosse Ehr' ward mir erkannt,

Ward heut' ich zum Spruchsprecher ernannt:

Und was mein Spruch euch künden soll,

Glaubt, das ist hoher Ehre voll!

Wenn ihr die Kunst so hoch schon ehrt,

Da galt es zu beweisen,

Dass, wer ihr selbst gar angehört,

Sie schätzt ob allen Preisen.

Ein Meister reich und hochgemuth,

Der will euch heut' das zeigen:

Sein Töchterlein, sein höchstes Gut,

Mit allem Hab und eigen,

Dem Singer, der im Kunstgesang

Vor allem Volk den Preis errang,

Als höchsten Preises Kron'

Er bietet das zum Lohn.

Darum so hört, und stimmet bei:

Die Werbung steht dem Dichter frei.

Ihr Meister, die ihr's euch getraut,

Euch ruf' ich's vor dem Volke laut:

Erwägt der Werbung selt'nen Preis,

Und wem sie soll gelingen,

Be sure a guileless heart is his;
  Pure love and music in it.
This crown 's of worth infinite,
And ne'er, in recent days or olden,
By any hand so highly holden.
  As by this maiden tender:
  Good fortune may it lend her!
Thus Nuremberg gives honor due
To Art and all her Masters too.

(Great stir among all present.—Sachs goes up to Pogner, who presses his hand, deeply moved.)

Pogner.
  O Sachs! my friend! what thanks I owe!
  How well my heart's distress you know!

Sachs.
  There 's much at stake! But care dispel!
(The Prentices have hastily heaped up before the platform of the Master-singers a little mound of turf, beaten it solid, and bestrewn it with flowers.)

Sachs. Now then, my Masters, if you're agreed,
  We will to our Trial-songs proceed.

Kothner.
          (Advancing.)
  Unmarried Masters, forward to win!
  Let him commence who 's most mature.—
  Friend Beckmesser, it is time! Begin!

Beckmesser.
(Quits the stand; the Prentices conduct him to the mound; he stumbles up to it, treads uncertainly, and totters.)
  The devil! How rickety! Make that secure!
    (The boys snigger, and beat the turf lustily.)

The People.
  (Severally, whilst Beckmesser is settling himself)

What! he to woo! Is n't he a fat one?
In the lady's place, I 'd not have that one!
  He cannot keep his feet:
  How will the man compete?
Be still! He 's quite a great professor:
That is the Town-clerk, Master Beckmesser.
  He 'll tumble soon.
  Old pantaloon!
Hush! leave off your jokes and prate;
He is a learned magistrate.

The Prentices.
      (Drawn up in order.)
  Silentium! Silentium!
  Make no sound — e'en the merest hum!

(Beckmesser, anxiously scanning all faces, makes a grand bow to Eva.)

Kothner. Now begin!

Dass er sich rein und edel weiss;
  Im Werben, wie im Singen,
  Will er das Reis erringen,
Dass nie bei neuen noch bei Alten
Ward je so herrlich hoch gehalten,
  Als von der lieblich Reinen,
  Die niemals soll beweinen.
Dass Nürnberg mit höchstem Werth
Die Kunst und ihre Meister ehrt.

(Grosse Bewegung unter Allen.—Sachs geht auf Pogner zu, der ihm gerührt die Hand drückt.)

Pogner.
  O Sachs! Mein Freund! Wie dankenswerth!
  Wie wisst ihr, was mein Herz beschwert!

Sachs.
  's war viel gewagt! Jetzt habt nur Muth!
(Die Lehrbuben haben vor der Meistersinger-Bühne schnell von Rasenstücken einen kleinen Hügel aufgeworfen, fest gerammelt, und reich mit Blumen überdeckt.)

Sachs.
  Nun denn, wenn's Meistern und Volk beliebt,
  Zum Wettgesang man den Anfang giebt.

Kothner.
         (Tritt vor.)
  Ihr ledig' Meister, macht euch bereit!
  Der Aeltest' sich zuerst anlässt: —
  Herr Beckmesser, ihr fangt an, 's ist Zeit!

Beckmesser.
(Verlässt die Singerbühne; die Lehrbuben führen ihn zu dem Blumenhügel: er strauchelt darauf, tritt unsicher und schwankt.)
  Zum Teufel! Wie wackelig! Macht das hübsch fest!
(Die Buben lachen unter sich und stopfen an dem Rasen.)

Das Volk.
(Unterschiedlich, während Beckmesser sich zurecht macht.)
  Wie, der? Der wirbt? Scheint mir nicht der Rechte!
An der Tochter Stell' ich den nicht möchte.
  Er kann nicht 'mal stehn:
  Wie wird's mit dem geh'n?
Seid still! 's ist gar ein tücht'ger Meister!
Stadtschreiber ist er: Beckmesser heisst er.
  Gott ist der dumm!
  Er fällt fast um!
Still! macht keinen Witz;
Der hat im Rathe Stimm' und Sitz.

Die Lehrbuben.
      (In Aufstellung.)
  Silentium! Silentium!
  Lasst all das Reden und Gesumm'!
(Beckmesser macht, ängstlich in ihren Blicken forschend, eine gezierte Verbeugung gegen Eva.)

Kothner.   Fanget an!

Beckmesser.

(Sings to his old melody, a vain attempt at Walter's song; his ornamental phrases being spoiled by continual failure of memory and increasing confusion.)

" Yawning and steaming with roseate light,
        My hair was filled
        With scent distilled,
    My boots were beaming
    With no meaning,
    The guard I did invite
        To strap me tight."

(After having settled his feet more securely, and taken a peep at the manuscript :)

" Oh for the claws of the guard for my hold!
        A flea looked down
        Upon my crown,
    My chest intending
    I suspending
    My weight from roots unrolled
        That furnished hold."

(He again tries to steady himself, and to correct himself by the manuscript.)

The Masters. What is the matter? Is he insane? His song's sheer nonsense, that is plain!

The People.
                (Louder.)
Charming wooer!   He 'll soon get his due:
Suspend on the gallows—that 's what he 'll do!

Beckmesser.
            (More and more confused.)
        " Get me a bride!
A lovely merry girl I sued —
Afraid, she could not score my face —
As sweet and fair as she was rude.
        Like to have died,
She shook me from her embrace;
        With white eyes glowing,
        Her hound was going
To stir my long legs as I found.
Such thunderous brutes surround
        The tree of tripe!"

(Here all burst into a peal of loud laughter.)

Beckmesser.

(Descends the mound and hastens to Sachs.)
Accursed cobbler!   This is through you!
That song is not my own, 't is true;
'T was Sachs, the idol of your throng,
Hans Sachs himself gave me the song!
The wretch, on purpose to abash,
Has palmed on me this sorry trash.

(He rushes away furiously, and disappears in the crowd. Great confusion.)

People.
Why!   How can that be?   'T is still more surprising!
That song by Sachs?   Our wonder is rising!

Beckmesser.

(Singt mit seiner Melodie, verkehrter Prosodie und mit süsslich verzierten Absätzen, öfters durch mangelhaftes Memoriren gänzlich behindert, und mit immer mehr wachsender ängstlicher Verwirrung.)

" Morgen ich leuchte in rosigem Schein
        Voll Blut und Duft
        Geht schnell die Luft; —
    Wohl bald gewonnen,
    Wie zerronnen, —
    Im Garten lud ich ein —
        Garstig und fein."

(Nachdem er sich mit den Füssen wieder gerichtet, und im Manuscript heimlich nachgelesen.)

    Wohn' ich erträglich im selbigen Raum,
        Hol' Gold und Frucht —
        Bleisaft und Wucht:
    Mich holt am Pranger —
    Der Verlanger, —
    Auf luft'ger Steige kaum —
        Häng' ich am Baum."

(Er sucht sich wieder zurecht zu stellen und im Manuscript zurecht zu finden.)

Die Meister.
Was soll das heissen? Ist er nun toll?
Sein Lied ist ganz von Unsinn voll!

Das Volk.
            (Immer lauter.)
Schöner Werber!   Der find't seinen Lohn:
Bald hängt er am Galgen; man sieht ihn schon.

Beckmesser.
            (Immer verwirrter.)
        " Heimlich mir graut —
Weil hier es munter will hergeh'n : —
An meiner Leiter stand ein Wieb,
Sie schämt' und wollt mich nicht beseh'n.
        Bleich wie ein Kraut —
Umfasert mir Hanf meinen Leib; —
        Die Augen zwinkend —
        Der Hund blies winkend —
Was ich vor langem verzehrt, —
Wie Frucht, so Holz und Pferd —
        Vom Leberbaum."

(Hier bricht Alles in schallendes Gelächter aus.)

Beckmesser.

(Verlässt wüthend den Hügel und eilt auf Sachs zu.)
Verdammter Schuster! Das dank' ich dir!
Das Lied, es ist gar nicht von mir:
Von Sachs, der hier so hoch verehrt,
Von eu'rem Sachs ward mir's bescheert!
Mich hat der Schändliche bedrängt,
Sein schlechtes Lied mir aufgehängt.

(Er stürzt wüthend fort und verliert sich unter dem Volke. Grosser Aufstand.)

Volk.
Mein!   Was soll das?   Jetzt wird's immer bunter!
Von Sachs das Lied?   Das nähm' uns doch Wunder!

Master-Singers.
Explain this, Sachs! What a disgrace!
Is that song yours? Most novel case!

Sachs.
(Who has quietly picked up the paper which Beckmesser threw away.)
That song, indeed, is not by me:
Friend Beckmesser's wrong as he can be.
I tell you, sirs, the work is fine;
But it is easy to divine
That Beckmesser has sung it wrong.
I am accused and must defend:
A witness let me bid attend! —
Is there one here who knows I'm right,
Let him appear before our sight!
(Walter advances from out the crowd. — General stir.)
Bear witness the song is not by me,
And prove to all that, in the plea
    I have advanced for it,
    I said but what was fit.

The Masters.
Ah, Sachs! You're very sly indeed! —
But you may for this once proceed.

Sachs.
It shews our rules are of excellence rare
If now and then exceptions they'll bear.

People. A noble witness, proud and bold!
Methinks he should some good unfold.

Sachs. Masters and people all agree
To give my witness liberty,
Sir Walter von Stolzing, sing the song!
You, Masters, see if he goes wrong.
    (He gives the Masters the paper to follow with.)

Prentices. All are intent, hushed is the hum;
So we need not call out Silentium!

Die Meistersinger.
Erklärt doch, Sachs! Welch ein Skandal!
Von euch das Lied? Welch eigner Fall!

Sachs.
(Der ruhig das Blatt, welches ihm Beckmesser hingeworfen, aufgehoben hat.)
Das Lied, fürwahr, ist nicht von mir:
Herr Beckmesser irrt, wie dort, so hier!
Ich sag' euch Herr'n, das Lied ist schön:
Nur ist's auf den ersten Blick zu erseh'n,
Dass Freund Beckmesser es entstellt.
Ich bin verklagt, und muss besteh'n:
Drum lasst meinen Zeugen mich auserseh'n! —
Ist Jemand hier, der Recht mir weiss,
Der tret' als Zeug' in diesen Kreis!
(Walther tritt aus dem Volke hervor. Allgemeine Bewegung.)
So zeuget, das Lied sei nicht von mir;
Und zeuget auch, dass, was ich hier
    Hab' von dem Lied gesagt,
    Zuviel nicht sei gewagt.

Die Meister.
Ei, Sachs! Gesteht, ihr seid gar fein! —
So mag's denn heut' geschehen sein.

Sachs. Der Regel Güte daraus man erwägt,
Dass sie auch 'mal 'ne Ausnahm' verträgt.

Das Volk. Ein guter Zeuge, schön und kühn!
Mich dünkt, dem kann 'was Gut's erblüh'n!

Sachs. Meister und Volk sind gewillt
Zu vernehmen, was mein Zeuge gilt.
Herr Walther von Stolzing, singt das Lied!
Ihr Meister, les't, ob's ihm gerieth.
    (Er giebt den Meistern das Blatt zum Nachlesen.)

Die Lehrbuben.
Alles gespannt, 's gibt kein Gesumm',
Da rufen wir auch nicht Silentium!

PRIZE SONG.

English Version by L. U.

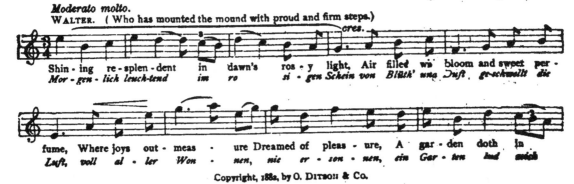

Moderato molto.
WALTER. (Who has mounted the mound with proud and firm steps.)

cres.

Shin - ing re - splen - dent in dawn's ros - y light, Air filled wa bloom and sweet per -
Mor - gen - lich leuch-tend im ro - si - gen Schein von Blüth' und Duft ge-schwellt die

fume, Where joys out - meas - ure Dreamed of pleas - ure, A gar - den doth in
Luft, voll al - ler Won - nen, nie er - son - nen, ein Gar - ten lud mich

un poco rit. con estasia.

vite. And there be-neath a mag-ic tree, Of fruits hung rich with treas-ure, In
ein, dort un-ter ei-nem Wun-der-baum, von Frück-ten reich be-han-gen, zu

bless-ed dream of love I see What ar-dent thirst for pleas-ure With prom-ise doth en-
schau'n in sel'-gem Lie-bes-traum, was höchs-tem Lust-ver-lan-gen Er-fül-lung kühn ver

dolce.

tice, The fair-est maid:.. E-va in Pa-ra-dise!
kiess, das schön-ste Weib:.. E-va im Pa-ra-dies!

Closed round by shad-ows, sur-round-ed by night, By path-way steep I reach a
A-bend-lich däm-mernd um-schloss mich die Nacht, auf stei-lem Pfad war ich ge-

deep And no-ble foun-tain on a moun-tain Whose waves smile on.... me
naht zu ei-ner Quel-le rei-ner Wel-le, die lo-ckend mir... ge-

p ritard.

bright. And there be-neath a lau-rel tree Through which the stars are gleam-ing, The
lacht: dort un-ter ei-nem Lor-beer-baum, von Ster-nen hell durch-schie-nen, ich

no-blest wom-an's form I see In wak-ing po-et dream-ing, While
schaut' im wa-chen Dich-ter-traum von hei-lig hol-den Mie-nen, mich

she with ho-ly, gra-cious mien My brow be-dews. Par-nas-sus' sa-cred
net-zend mit dem e-dlen Nass, das hehr-ste Weib, die Mu-se des Par-

con molto fuoco.

muse! Most bless-ed day When I from po-et's dream a-
nass! Huld-reich-ster Tag dem ich aus Dichter's Traum er-

wake! Now what I dreamed of Pa-ra-dise, Di-vine in fresh-er glo-ry, lies
wacht! das ich er-träumt, das Pa-ra-dies, in himmlisch neu ver-klär-ter Pracht,

Be-fore my eyes, While smil-ing still the foun-tain shows the way, The
hell vor mir lag, da-hin la-chend nun der Quell den Pfad mir wies, die

maid E - lys - ian I saw in - vis - ion, She whom my heart doth
dort ge - bo - ren, mein Herz er - ko - ren, der Er - de lieb - lich - stes

choose, Earth's fair - est, and my muse, So ho - - ly, grave, and good, By
Bild, als Mu - se mir ge - weiht, so hei - - lig ernst als mild, ward

me is bold - ly wooed, Here by the day's bright sun, By
kühn von mir ge - freit; am lich - ten Tag der Son - nen, durch

Poco. Rit.

power of song is won Par - nas - - - sus and Pa - ra - dise!"
San - ges Sieg ge - won - nen Par - nass und Pa - ra - dies!"

People. Give him the prize!	**Volk.** Reich' ihm das Reis!
Maiden, rise!	Sein der Preis!
No one could woo in nobler wise!	Keiner wie er zu werben weiss!
Masters. Yes, glorious singer! Victor, rise!	**Die Meister.** Ja, holder Sänger! Nimm das Reis!
Your song has won the Master-prize!	Dein Sang erwarb dir Meisterpreis!
Pogner. O Sachs! All this I owe to you:	**Pogner.** O Sachs! Dir dank' ich Glück und Ehr',
My happiness revives anew.	Vorüber nun all' Herzbeschwer!

(Eva, who from the commencement of the scene has preserved a calm composure, and has seemed wrapt from all that passed around, has listened to Walter immovably; but now, when at the conclusion both Masters and people express their involuntary admiration, she rises, advances to the edge of the platform and places on the brow of Walter, who kneels on the steps, a wreath of myrtle and laurel, whereupon he rises and she leads him to her father, before whom they both kneel. Pogner extends his hands in benediction over them.)

(Eva, die von Anfang des Auftrittes her in sicherer, ruhiger Haltung verblieben, und bei allen Vorgängen wie in seliger Geistesentrücktheit sich erhalten, hat Walther unverwandt zugehört; jetzt, während am Schlusse des Gesanges Volk und Meister, gerührt und ergriffen, unwillkürlich ihre Zustimmung ausdrücken, erhebt sie sich, schreitet an den Rand der Singerbühne, und drückt auf die Stirn Walthers, welcher zu den Stufen herangetreten ist und vor ihr sich niedergelassen hat, einen aus Lorbeer und Myrthen geflochtenen Kranz, worauf dieser sich erhebt und von ihr zu ihrem Vater geleitet wird, vor welchem Beide niederknieen; Pogner streckt segnend seine Hände über sie aus.)

Sachs.	**Sachs.**
(Pointing to the group.)	(Deutet dem Volke mit der Hand auf die Gruppe.)
My witness answered not amiss!	Den Zeugen, denk' es, wählt' ich gut;
Do you find fault with me for this?	Tragt ihr Hans Sachs drum üblen Muth?
People.	**Volk.**
(Jubilantly.)	(Jubelnd.)
Hans Sachs! No! It was well devised!	Hans Sachs! Nein! Das war schön erdacht'
Your tact you 've once more exercised!	Das habt ihr einmal wieder gut gemacht!
Several Master-Singers.	**Mehrere Meistersinger.**
Now, Master Pogner! As you should,	Auf, Meister Pogner! Euch zum Ruhm,
Give him the honor of Masterhood!	Meldet dem Junker sein Meisterthum.
Pogner.	**Pogner.**
(Bringing forward a gold chain with three medallions.)	(Eine goldene Kette mit drei Denkmünzen tragend.)
Receive kind David's likeness true:	Geschmückt mit König David's Bild,
The Master's Guild is free to you.	Nehm' ich euch auf in der Meister Gild'.

Walter.

(Shrinking back involuntarily.)
A Master! Nay!
I'll find reward some other way!

(The Masters look disconcertedly towards Sachs.)

Sachs.

(Grasping Walter by the hand.)
Disparage not the Master's ways,
But show respect to Art!
So heed my words:—
Honor your German Masters
If you would stay disasters!
For while they dwell in every heart,
Though should depart
The pride of holy Rome,
Still thrives at home
Our sacred German Art!

(All join enthusiastically in the last verse.—Eva takes the crown from Walter's head and places it on Sachs's; he takes the chain from Pogner's hand and puts it round Walter's neck.— Walter and Eva lean against Sachs, one on each side: Pogner sinks on his knee before him as if in homage. The Master-singers point to Sachs, with outstretched hands, as to their chief. While the Prentices clap hands and shout and dance, the people wave hats and 'kerchiefs in enthusiasm.)

All. Hail Sachs! Hans Sachs!
Hail Nuremberg's darling Sachs!

(The Curtains falls.)

Walther.

(Zuckt unwillkürlich heftig zurück.)
Nicht Meister! Nein!
Will ohne Meister selig sein!
(Die Meister blicken in grosser Betretenheit auf Sachs.)

Sachs.

(Walther fest bei der Hand fassend.)
Verachtet mir die Meister nicht,
Und ehrt mir ihre Kunst!
Drum sag' ich Euch:
Ehrt eure deutschen Meister,
Dann bannt ihr gute Geister!
Und gebt ihr ihrem Wirken Gunst,
Zerging' in Dunst
Das heil'ge röm'sche Reich
Uns bliebe gleich
Die heil'ge deutsche Kunst!

(Alle fallen begeistert in den Schlussvers ein. Eva nimmt den Kranz von Walther's Stirn und drückt ihn Sachs auf; dieser nimmt die Kette aus Pogner's Hand, und hängt sie Walther um, Walther und Eva lehnen sich zu beiden Seiten an Sachsen's Schultern; Pogner lässt sich, wie huldigend, auf ein Knie vor Sachs nieder. Die Meistersinger deuten mit erhobenen Händen auf Sachs, als auf ihr Haupt. Während die Lehrbuben jauchzend in die Hände schlagen und tanzen, schwenkt das Volk begeistert Hüte und Tücher.)

Volk.

Heil Sachs! Hans Sachs!
Heil Nürnberg's theurem Sachs!

(Der Vorhang fällt.)

CPSIA information can be obtained
at www.ICGtesting.com
Printed in the USA
BVHW011802281121
622723BV00003B/29